Early Pleasures & Pastimes

Bobbie Kalman

The Early Settler Life Series

 Crabtree Publishing Company

To Blanka and Clarissa

A special thanks to the following people without whose help this book would not have been possible:

Senior editor: *Lise Gunby*
Researcher and editor: *Susan Hughes*
Assistant editors: *Mary Ann Horgan*
 Carla Williams
 Maria Protz
Freelance editor: *Dan Liebman*
Design and mechanicals: *Nancy Cook*
Photographers: *Sarah Peters*
 Stephen Mangione
 Donna Acheson
Picture researchers: *Linda Kudo*
 Noel Rutland
Librarians: *Margaret Crawford Maloney*
 Dana Tenny
 Jill Shefrin
 Stanley Triggs

A thank you to Arnie Krause for keeping us on schedule

Cataloging in Publication Data

Kalman, Bobbie, 1947 –
 Early Pleasures and Pastimes

(Early settler life series)
Includes index.
ISBN 0-86505-025-2 hardcover
ISBN 0-86505-024-4 softcover

1. Recreation – History. 2. Amusements – History.
I. Title. II. Series.

GV45.K34 1983 790'.9'03

102 Torbrick Avenue
Toronto M4J 4Z5

350 Fifth Avenue
Suite 3308
New York, N.Y. 10001

Contents

The imagination provided endless hours of pleasure. Each story supplied daydreams about faraway places. Daydreams led to games of pretend and more stories to be shared.

Imagine!

If you were asked to write down some of your favorite pleasures, how would you start? Would you list the most exciting or funny TV programs? Would you talk about the video games that you enjoy playing? Would you start humming the latest hit song?

Suppose someone took away all the video games, computers, television sets, bicycles, stereos, and gadgets. Suppose they told you that you could only play after your chores were done, and never on Sundays. Suppose you shared a room with your parents, brothers and sisters, and a grandparent or two. How do you imagine you would feel in such a situation?

At first, you would probably feel frustrated. You might feel lost without the machines you depend on to provide your fun. However, before too long, you would discover that people are far more exciting than television sets and electronic games!

The value of friendship

The settlers' world of fun was founded on human relationships. Friendship was one of the settlers' highest values in life. Once there was friendship, the imagination provided the **pleasures and pastimes.** Out of caring, sharing, and cooperation came a wonderful world of pleasure that no gadget today could possibly replace.

Let yourself be taken back in time by the pages of this book. Discover what it's like to have your pleasures supplied by your very own built-in video game, your **imagination.**

Grandfather's apples are the sweetest!

Simple pleasures

The settlers found pleasure in the simple things in life: the smell of homemade bread, the sight of the first bloom in spring, the sound of a babbling brook. Every tree and stone on the settler homestead had a special meaning to the people who lived there. If the trees could talk, they would probably tell stories of children skipping rope, of women quilting in the shade, of young men arm-wrestling for the title of village champion!

Settler children used to claim that their grandmother's jam was the sweetest, their grandfather's fruit the juiciest, their mother's garden filled with the most colorful flowers imaginable. The beauty of unspoiled nature was a daily pleasure to the senses of the settlers.

The settlers sat together around one candle to read, sew, and talk. Mother trims the wick. Grandfather is enjoying catching up on world news. Soon he must pass the paper on to the next neighbor.

Cosy around the fire

The home was the center of early settler life. Settler families spent their happiest times under their own roof, talking and laughing around the fireplace. There is something about a fireplace that makes us feel cosy and secure. The settlers must have had those same feelings as they gathered around their kitchen fireplace after dinner each night. In the early settler homes the fire provided the only light after dark. What kind of activities do you like to play in the evenings? The settlers had nothing else to do but share the day's experiences or listen to grandfather talk about the days when he was a young boy. Even after the settlers had candles, they sat in one room reading, sewing, or playing. The family was very close in those days. Parents spent every evening with their children. One of the biggest joys of life was being with people you loved.

Catherine tries to make her turkey trot. Do you think this was a good way to travel?

Tabby looks a little worried as the girls juggle her babies. The birth of new kittens was always an exciting event in the settler household.

Barnyard fun

Outside the settler house there were many things to enjoy. The barn was a great place for playing hide-and-seek, reading a good book, or just relaxing in a pile of straw. Hunting for eggs that the chickens had laid all around the yard was a real challenge! Milking the family cow was also no easy feat, especially when there were flies buzzing around your nose, and old Betsy's tail was swatting your ear!

The barnyard animals were very special to the settlers. These animals provided work, milk, food, and even companionship! It was always exciting when eggs were about to hatch into chicks or ducklings. The whole settler household would wait anxiously for a new calf or foal to be born. Baby pigs and goats were also fun to have around. Witnessing the miracle of new life was a regular happening in the settler household. It is a joyful event that simply has no equal! Have you ever seen a cat or a hamster having babies?

Not all the barnyard animals were fun. Chubby has dug up the garden once too often!

The garden wheelbarrow is just the right size for Mary. Mark gives his sister a rocky ride, but Mary is determined to sit tight.

John loves to swing on the garden gate, but he must head off to school or he'll be late.

Mother gave Sammy his very own seeds to grow. He weeded and watered, and to his surprise, the plants actually came up!

Gardens of delight

The settlers took pride in their orchards and gardens. It was a custom to take guests outside to show them the garden. The garden was usually split in two with a walkway down the middle and paths around the outside. Flowers were planted on one side and herbs and vegetables on the other. Did you know that about two hundred years ago the settlers planted tomatoes among the flowers? In the early days people thought that tomatoes were beautiful to look at, but extremely poisonous to eat. Children were not allowed near them. The settlers called tomatoes **love-apples**, probably because of their heart-like shape.

Some of the other simple pleasures found on the settler homestead were swinging on the gate, getting a ride in the wheelbarrow, pumping an ice-cold glass of water from the well, shouting down a rain barrel, and skinny-dipping in the pond. There was always a river or lake nearby where children fished or caught frogs and pollywogs.

The school yard was the neighborhood playground. Children stayed after school to play tag, marbles, and ball games. Ruth watches as she waits for her turn on the seesaw. It looks as though Elisabeth will jump off. Poor Heather. Hope she has a soft landing!

Exploring the community

The settlers found many ways to have fun at home, but for a change of scenery they met with neighbors at other places in the community. The school yard was always a good spot to meet friends for a game of tug-of-war or a ride on the seesaw. The blacksmith shop was a lively place where people gathered to tell stories or listen to a tune on the fiddle. The blacksmith was often happy to take time out for a quick game of horseshoes. He always had the proper equipment on hand!

See you at the store!

The busiest meeting place in the village for both adults and children was the general store. Men gathered by the potbelly stove to chat over a cosy game of checkers. Women exchanged stories, collected the mail, and caught up on the latest fashion trends. Children could not resist the tempting candy jars. The general store was usually full of settlers enjoying one another's company. The storekeeper appreciated both the company and the business.

Matthew cannot choose between the two flavors of candy. Peppermint or lemon? These two friends meet at the store every day to buy a piece of candy.

When the miller's away, the children will play! The mill wheel was a great place for training future acrobats. Children were warned not to play near the mill wheel when it was turning to grind grain. However, it was hard to resist the challenging climb when the wheel was not in action.

The mill pond was too deep for this non-swimmer!

The miller is surprised that Jill weighs so much. "Gosh, you are growing fast!" he says. Then he discovers that Billy is leaning on the scales.

Milling around

The gristmill provided many opportunities for fun. There was usually a pond beside the mill which was great for fishing or swimming. The mill wheel, when not in use, was a challenging climb. If you were curious about your weight, the miller might agree to weigh you on the mill scales. Do you think you would weigh as much as a sack of grain? After dark, the mill was a good place to tell ghost stories.

The ghost of the mill

There is an old story about a group of boys who were fishing in the mill pond one evening after sunset. The mill wheel was still and the boys were quiet so they would not frighten the fish away. One of the boys was slightly bored. Looking around, he happened to glance in the direction of a window on the top floor of the mill. Suddenly, a white ghost appeared in the window! The boy screamed. He and the others dropped their poles and ran for their lives.

From then on, children in that village dared each other to stay after dark and witness the ghost. Many children must have seen it. What they did not realize, however, was that the scary white figure was no ghost. Can you guess what it was? It was the miller, covered in flour!

11

The pleasures of family life

Many settler families were large. They included parents and children, often an aunt or two, uncles, and at least one grandparent. It was difficult to feel bored with so many people in the house. Although everyone had to work hard, including the children, there were many pleasures for the family members to share.

Mothers made dolls for their daughters. Girls learned to sew and knit by the age of five, so they were able to design and make their own doll clothes. Girls also practiced sewing different stitches on their samplers. They stitched Bible verses and pictures. The finished samplers were framed and hung on the wall.

Fathers and sons fashioned toys from wood. They made small wheelbarrows, sleds, carts, blocks, and wooden animals. Settler children thought that playing with toys they had made themselves was double the pleasure! Making the toy was just as much fun as playing with it!

Role playing

In the early days, boys and girls did not play with the same toys. Girls were expected to play with toys that prepared them to become good mothers. Boys played games that prepared them to work at jobs outside the home, such as farming, medicine, crafts, and storekeeping. Settler children were restricted to traditional roles. Boys and girls nowadays enjoy the same kinds of amusements because when they grow up they have many careers to choose from. Men and women can do the same types of work. What kind of work would you like to do when you grow up?

A sense of belonging

Grandmothers and grandfathers were a good source of entertainment for settler children. They read to the children and told exciting adventure stories about faraway places. Grandparents gave their grandchildren a solid feeling of family and roots. They provided the children with a sense of who they were. Grandmother would say, "Sarah, you are just like your great-grandmother Laura Wilson. She was spirited and just as stubborn." Or she would say, "Joshua, you're as clever with your hands as your great-uncle Samuel. Why, there wasn't a piece of wood around that he could not whittle into something useful!" Hearing these comparisons made the children feel that they belonged to a very special family.

Dr. Jimmy makes a house call. Do you think Jim will find a pulse? He has borrowed Father's watch to help him with the diagnosis.

These sisters are good mothers to their dolls. Most settler girls grew up to be mothers. There were not many jobs for women then.

Grandmother is a patient teacher because she loves her student. Sarah will soon be able to knit her own scarf and mitts.

Scott imitates his grandfather by reading the farm news. Scott is still too small to fill Grandfather's slippers.

13

The settlers did not have a chance to see their relatives very often. The Anderson family, together for a reunion, kept in touch the rest of the year through their family circular.

Family circulars

Relatives often settled in different parts of the country. They could not see each other as often as they wanted. To keep a sense of family, some settlers started family circulars. On the first day of each month, a member of the family would take a few sheets of paper, fill part of a page with news from that family, and then mail the pages to a sister or a cousin. The family who received the news would then add its own news and mail the papers to another family member. In this way, the family news traveled once a month to each member of an extended family. All the circulars were collected by one family member, perhaps the grandmother, who later gave it to the grandchildren as a family history.

Some families kept journals based on the same idea as the circular. On Monday, for example, Mother wrote about her day. On Tuesday, Father added a page on the latest farming or village news. On Wednesday, a brother or sister made an entry about a day at school, and so on. By keeping a journal, each member of the family was aware of the activities and feelings of the others. Maybe your family would like to start a circular or a family journal. In a few years' time, it would be fun to read it again!

Fred is lucky to have such a fascinated audience! His sister will also play a musical instrument when she grows up. Will she choose drums?

Household harmony

Music was as important to the settlers as it is to us. There were no radios or record players then, but many people played musical instruments and everyone sang and danced. Music was also an important part of family life. One of the first expensive additions to the settler household was a piano. One family member taught the others how to play. Sometimes music teachers traveled from house to house teaching children to play musical instruments. A teacher would stay with one family for a month and then with another, eventually returning to the first to pick up where the last lesson left off. Would you like your music teacher to live in your house for a month? You would have to be sure to practice every day!

The music teacher has come to hear Jane's lessons. Now Jane wishes she had practiced more!

These talented brothers and sisters are popular at parties and dances. They can all sing and play instruments.

In new settlements, people did not have time to build a church until after they finished their own homes. Until they could build a church, they held services in their homes. This circuit priest traveled from settlement to settlement to conduct Sunday Mass.

Religion was an important part of the daily life of the settlers. These Roman Catholic settlers, hard at work on the harvest, stop at noon to say a prayer called the **Angelus.**

Keeping their faith

The settlers were grateful for their success in the New World. They offered prayers of thanks for each day of happiness. They asked God's help to stay healthy and strong.

Sunday was a special day for the settlers. It was a day of rest and prayer for adults and children alike. Sunday was reserved for reading the Bible. Bible stories gave the settlers advice in times of trouble and examples of courage and resourcefulness. There was only one toy children were allowed to play with on Sundays. This was the Noah's Ark, a model boat made of wood which contained pairs of animals. The story of Noah is told in the Bible. By playing with the ark, the children learned a religious lesson.

Parting words

As communities grew, settlers built churches. Adults attended church services while children went to Sunday school. When the service was over, everyone gathered in front of the church to greet one another and exchange news. The settlers discussed the latest births, marriages, and deaths. They talked about the condition of the roads and the weather. They compared the prices of wheat, produce, and lumber. After this friendly visiting, the families headed home for Sunday dinner. Young men waited at the church door and offered to "see home" their favorite girls.

Methodist meetings

Several times a year, social events, such as potluck dinners, were held at the church. In the summer months, the Methodists held camp meetings in meadows or clearings. These meetings were a good way to bring people of the same faith together. The meetings also gave these Methodist settlers a chance to enjoy one another's company. The open-air assemblies with their lively bands of music drew great crowds and sometimes lasted up to two weeks at a time. People of all ages and often of different faiths gathered to take part or just to watch!

It was sometimes difficult to keep your mind on the service when your favorite beau sat just across the aisle.

Church choirs spent many hours practicing the Sunday hymns. Bill prefers to practice his charms instead of his singing.

Warmth, food, drink, and music welcomed these cold visitors!

"Surprise! Surprise! The party is at your house tonight!"

Mr. Johnson and his friends enjoy swapping tales of the early days in this country.

All visitors welcome

Just seeing another human being was a pleasure for the settlers. It provided a break from the loneliness of backwoods life. The settlers always kept their doors open to anyone who needed a place to stay. Settlers always had food on hand to offer unexpected guests. Sometimes guests stayed overnight. Winter was the busiest visiting season, because travel by sleigh over snow was easy. In the other seasons, the roads were either muddy or bumpy. In many cases, the visitors who came to call were strangers looking for warmth.

Calling on friends

In later days, as villages grew into towns, visiting became a more formal affair. Some people visited friends on a certain day each week. The callers were sure that their friends expected many visitors because this was their "at home" day. The visitors were usually entertained in the parlor. The hostess served tea, coffee, sandwiches, and cakes. The settlers had calling cards printed with their names on them. They left a calling card with their hosts after a visit. This helped the hosts to keep a record of their guests. If a visitor called on a friend or neighbor and that person was not home, the caller left a card in the front hall of the house. When the absent friend returned she would know who had called while she was out.

Surprise parties

Settlers often organized surprise parties for their friends. Seven or eight families prepared food and drinks. They met at the nearest crossroads. When everyone had assembled, the whole party proceeded to the home of the family for whom the party was planned. The guests poured in the door carrying food and drinks, and with a few musicians in tow. The furniture was pushed back against the walls and the dancing began. After the party was over, the guests helped to clean the house before going home. Wouldn't you like to open your front door and find all your friends ready to give you a party at your house?

19

Lunch time for the "hive!" Only a chance to get their picture taken could momentarily distract the hungry workers from their meal! Try to imagine what kind of bee these settlers have organized. Do the trees in the background give you a clue?

Harvesting was hard work, but it made the midday break all the more welcome. Little Sally and her mother have come out to visit Father. They can only stay a short time because they must return home to finish preparing food for the threshing bee tomorrow!

When the work is done, it's time for fun!

An important social occasion in settler life was the **bee** or work party. Bees were organized to complete difficult tasks, such as building homes, barns, and churches. The settlers in an area came to help a neighboring family with jobs that were impossible for one family to do alone. The settler family that organized a bee was expected to return the help by working at other bees in the neighborhood.

Harvest happenings

In the fall, young men and women got together to peel and string pumpkins and apples for drying. When paring apples, they took special care to ensure that the skin would come off in one long piece. They twirled the paring up in the air and let it fall. It often resembled a letter of the alphabet when it dropped to the floor. This letter was supposed to be the initial of the future husband or wife of the person who had thrown the peel.

Husking bees were also common in the fall. The settlers assembled in a barn to husk corn. Men and women sat in alternate seats. When one of the men found a colored ear of corn, he was allowed to kiss the girl or woman next to him. Some young men came with one or two ears of red corn hidden in their pockets, eager to claim the kiss of their favorite young woman.

I dare you ...

Settlers finished their day of work with trials of strength, such as wrestling, jumping, stone-putting or wrestling a bear cub. Sometimes there were feats of daring. Men might eat a handful of frozen ants from a maple stump or suck up to forty raw eggs at a sitting. Would you like to accept these dares? What a way to spoil your appetite!

Would you dare to wrestle this bear?

Settlers who called a bee provided food and drinks for the helpers. There was plenty to eat and drink during the day, but when the work ended, the serious eating began. There were heaping plates full of food laid out on long tables. Eating was a big part of the entertainment at a bee.

Dancing the night away

The bees usually ended in dancing. After a huge supper, which was served buffet style, the settlers' toes started a-tapping. The "music," as some would call it, was furnished by a popular local musician who played the fiddle. If there was no fiddler at the dance, the musicians used a zither or a paper-covered comb. Music was also made with spoons, tin kettles, and pokers and tongs. Music or noise? Sometimes it was hard to tell! The settlers danced reels, jigs, and their favorite dance, the square dance, until dawn.

These two couples thought they could find more adventure on a hike. They climbed hills, balanced on logs to cross a waterfall, and made their own path through the forest. Hope they find their way back to the picnic before all the food is gone!

Meanwhile ... back at the picnic the others enjoy the food, as well as the company.

Let's pack a picnic

After the first hard years of settlement, the settlers had more time to enjoy themselves. Picnics were a favorite pastime. Practical settlers combined picnics with fishing or berry-picking.

In later years, picnics were all play and no work. For those who preferred a little more excitement, excursions into the mountains or forests provided challenging outings. Tea meetings, oyster suppers, garden parties, and strawberry festivals were other opportunities for outdoor get-togethers.

A morning of picking berries often ended in an afternoon picnic. Maggie and Patricia proudly show off the "fruits of their labor."

23

The early settlers made their own Christmas entertainment by acting out **charades** *and* **pantomimes** *in their homes. In later days pantomimes were presented in theaters. Melanie is fascinated by the spectacle. This is the first time she has ever seen real actors on stage.*

Christmas, the social season

The snow made travel by sleigh easy, so the Christmas season meant many visits to and from the homes of family and friends. Pleasures were more important than presents. Children were treated to small presents, but gift-giving was not a very important part of Christmas. Settlers considered gifts of love more important. They shared food and clothing with the poor families in the community.

Bag and stick

One of the most popular parlor games was Blindman's Buff (see p. 75). An especially good game for a Christmas party was **Bag and Stick**. A paper bag was filled with candies and hung on a string from the ceiling. A player was blindfolded and turned around and around until he had completely lost his bearings. Then he was given a stick and told that he may have a certain number of shots at the bag of sweets. It was hard for the player to hit the bag when he was dizzy and confused. If the player missed the bag, the game continued with another player. The bag of sweets was finally broken with a fierce wallop. All the candies scattered onto the floor and everyone joined in the mad scramble to scoop them up. Can you think of another country where a game like Bag and Stick is played? What is the name of the container in which the candy is hidden?

Food for thought

On Christmas Day, dinner was a feast. Out came all the treats that the settlers had been preparing for weeks. The wonderful smells and the warm food drew everyone to the huge dining table. After Christmas dinner many people went to church. Do you celebrate Christmas in a different way? Many people do not recognize Christmas as a holiday. Perhaps you do not. The traditions of the early settlers are certainly not the only ones celebrated in this country. We must be sure to remember that many other people from other parts of the world brought with them their own special celebrations in later years.

"Let's all join hands to welcome in the New Year. We are lucky to be healthy and with friends on this joyous occasion. May God bless us all in the year to come."

The muffled bells are ringing. Any moment now, we will hear ... DING, DONG, DING, DONG!

Ringing in the New Year

On New Year's Eve, the settlers who lived in a town or near a church could hear the muffled church bells ring out the old year. Everyone knew when it was midnight because the loud sounds of the bells greeted the new year with joyful noise.

The settlers celebrated the new year with parties and visiting. All disagreements and bad feelings were forgotten. Everyone was friendly! Many early settlers exchanged gifts on New Year's Day. The gifts were handmade and suited especially to the child who was to receive them. How wonderful it was to begin the new year with new toys! Soon customs changed and gifts were given on Christmas Day.

The Hughes family is having a traditional "at home" New Year's Day. Instead of calling on families individually, this group of young men decided to get together and sing carols to the families they visit. Paul, the youngest caller, has the voice of an angel. He will soon be rewarded with some cider and perhaps some sandwiches.

Wishing friends a Happy New Year

As towns grew larger, people continued the tradition of visiting on New Year's Day. Some people in the cities even advertised in the newspaper that they would be "at home" on New Year's Day. This meant that they were ready to entertain guests and offer food and drinks. Unfortunately, some bad-mannered men turned the tradition of visiting friends on New Year's Day into a game. They drove from home to home in a carriage, racing to see how many houses they could visit in a day. They rushed into houses when they had not even been invited, and ate and drank the refreshments of their reluctant hosts. "At home" advertisements disappeared because of these contests. Only close friends and relatives would meet to celebrate the new year.

While the men callers pay attention to Joan, little Joy only has eyes for her new blocks!

27

Mumming, a costumed custom

These mummers have worked hard on their costumes. Look carefully at the monster and the horse. Can you unravel these mysterious disguises? Which famous story are the mummers acting out?

Brian is not old enough to be a mummer this year but he likes to hide behind the mask his father made for the mumming parade.

The settlers brought the tradition of **mumming** from Europe. During Christmas week each year, families worked hard to create costumes for mumming parades. It was great fun searching for materials for costumes. These included old patched clothes, rags, sheets, blankets, and quilts. Some people even came disguised in their neighbor's clothes.

When New Year's Day arrived, the mummers put on as many clothes as possible in order to disguise their shapes and fool their friends. Some mummers blackened their faces with burnt cork or tar. Others painted their faces or covered them with veils. Masks made of cardboard, paper, or cloth made especially good disguises. Ropes for hair and sheep tails for whiskers were added. Some mummers attached animal heads or horns to the headdresses of their costumes to make them even more bizarre!

Mum's the word!

When ready, the mummers met and paraded down the streets of the town. They usually visited the Town Hall first and then the homes of other settlers who tried hard to guess the identities of their masked guests. How strange it must have been not to recognize even a close friend or one's own cousin! Guessing a mummer's identity was especially difficult because the mummers also tried to change their voices! Often the mummers refused to speak at all. This is where the expression "keeping mum" comes from.

The unidentified entertainers

While the guessing was going on, the mummers entertained the household by singing, dancing, or playing musical instruments. Sometimes the mummers performed a play. The play always contained a fight in which a champion was killed and then miraculously revived by a doctor. The words to the play were not written down but were passed on from actor to actor.

When the host was finally able to identify the mummer, the mummer took his mask off. The last mummer to be recognized was very proud of his costume! The mummers were offered food and drinks in return for the pleasure they had given the household. Sometimes the captain of the mumming party asked for a small donation of money. At the end of the rounds, the mummers gave a ball with the money they had received.

Judgment day

Children were visited by mummers who were called "inquisitors." The adults knew who the disguised mummers were but the children were frightened by the "strangers" in their weird costumes. The inquisitors judged the children's behavior during the past year. They forced the children to answer questions about their misdeeds. The guilty children shook with fear! They were sorry they had misbehaved the year before. The inquisitors punished the bad children. The mummers usually convinced the frightened children to be obedient and responsible in the future. The good children in the family were praised by the strange visitors. Some of them were even given gifts.

Mumming was outlawed several times because the mummers, who felt protected by their disguises, also felt free to break the law. Despite laws against them, mummers kept appearing every New Year's Day. Although mumming is not as popular now as it was when the settlers first arrived, it is still enjoyed in a few parts of the country.

Old Mrs. Beezley does not look too pleased! She has just caught young Mr. Kent alone with Amanda! Mrs. Beezley is Amanda's chaperone and is very, very annoyed. In fact, she is so angry that she does not realize that she might be run over by the train if she does not move from the tracks.

Young people sometimes went to great extremes to avoid their chaperones. This young couple hid in a field of corn. It is hard to see them, isn't it? Will the chaperone find them? If she does, will they have a corny story to tell her?

Three's company!

Chaperones were paid to mind the business of other people. Families who could afford chaperones hired them to babysit their teenagers! When a young man asked a girl on a date, her chaperone was also invited, whether the young man liked it or not. When a girl entertained her beau in the parlor, the chaperone did not budge from the room.

A chaperone was a bit of a private eye. She investigated the backgrounds of the gentlemen who called on her charge to see which one would make the best match.

The chaperone could make courtship a miserable business. Some chaperones had soft hearts and helped young lovers to meet. Chaperones could be a nuisance, but they could also be a good excuse for avoiding unwanted courtship.

Millie is the storekeeper's daughter. While the storekeeper was busy, Jeremy took the opportunity to whisper sweet things into Millie's ear.

31

Bernadette and Samuel have arrived at the ferry at the same time, four days in a row. Could this be a coincidence, or do you think they planned to meet each other?

Country courtship

Young couples enjoyed simple pleasures. They walked, rode horseback, and took drives together in the young man's dogcart. Sleigh rides could be very romantic!

Sunday was the special day for courtship or **sparking.** A love-struck young man waited outside the church door to ask a young lady if he might "see her home." Young people also met at work bees. After the day's work was done, the reward was a party.

The spark of romance

Settlers held sparking bees just for fun. Men and women got together to find out more about each other. They talked, danced, and played games. One of their favorite games was played with a button. A large button made of bone was passed from hand to hand. A young girl was chosen to guess who had the button. If she pointed at the wrong person, the punishment was called "jail." She had to sit on a young man's knees. Some people thought the punishment was a pleasure!

Sprees and spooning

Everyone from babies to grandparents met at country dances called "sprees." Couples jigged, reeled, and square danced. The fiddler kept the dancers hopping until dawn. Good square dancers had sharp ears and quick feet. They followed the directions of the caller of the dance. Here is an example of the directions:

Ladies in the center,
  Gents take a walk,
Do-si-do and pass her by,
  Don't be shy.
Balance to the next and all swing out,
Gents hook on, ladies bounce back,
You get a shovel and I'll get a hoe,
Join your hands and circle half.
  Partners swing,
Right and left back to the same old thing,
Around the hall, gents, take your own little gal
  For a promenade.
Stand her by and swing to the next,
Then bring her back with a half galopade.

At city soirées everyone was dressed to impress everyone else.

Have you ever square-danced? The directions are in a code. You have to learn the code before you can dance the square.

Between dances, couples nestled together like spoons. **Spooning** became a popular word for courtship.

Sweet talking

Conversation lozenges were sometimes given out to courting couples at bees and dances. These lozenges were heart-shaped candies with messages printed on them such as "Oh, how I pine for you!" or "Will you be my sweetheart?" If a boy presented a girl with a conversation lozenge and she did not throw it back at him, the romance was on its way. A candy with "Can I see you home?" might have been exchanged for one saying, "You are the boy of my heart!"

Sophisticated soirées

Town dances were more formal than country dances. Town dances were usually held in large dance halls or ballrooms rather than in homes. People arrived at these **soirées** well-groomed and wearing the latest fashions. An impressive orchestra supplied the music as the couples waltzed gracefully around the dance floor. Sparkling champagne and burgundy were served to the guests. The soirée included an abundant supper, and many extras such as tea, coffee, cakes, nuts, and raisins. If settlers could not afford to buy tickets to the soirée, they **bartered** for them. They traded eggs, butter, or vegetables in exchange for tickets.

33

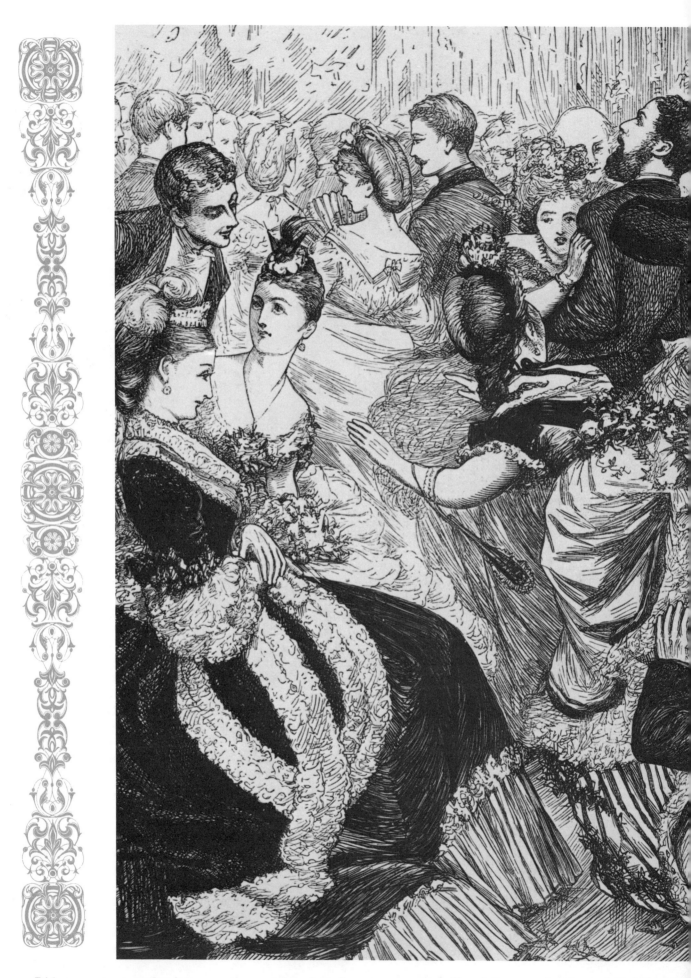

Did you ever wonder how women managed to dance so gracefully while wearing long full dresses?

George accidentally stepped on Florence's skirt. The dancers around them began to fall like dominoes.

Julia is both beautiful and charming. That is why she has so many suitors. On Valentine's Day she receives many cards. Although she does not care for anyone special, Julia is fond of each of her beaus. In her mind, she imagines keeping them all on a string!

36

A special day of love

Valentine's Day warmed up the settlers' winter. February 14 was the day to send a special message to a sweetheart. As Valentine's Day became more popular, it was celebrated with parties and costume balls. The guests with the most beautiful costumes were awarded prizes.

The settlers made their own valentine cards to give to their friends. They cut hearts out of paper and decorated packages or small gifts, hoping that their love tokens would please their sweethearts. Valentine's Day cards were delivered by hand before there was a regular mail service. Excited young people rushed to their door to see how many cards had been pushed under it. Sometimes they opened the door and found a love token hanging from the doorknob.

Paying for the right saying

Some young men felt it was impossible to find the right words for their valentine cards. In this case, a worried boyfriend could rush out to buy a "writer." A writer was a booklet that contained dozens of valentine verses and messages. The troubled boyfriend could search through it until he found just the right words and then copy them onto the valentine card he had made. If his sweetheart was pleased with his message, the lucky young man often did not find it necessary to tell his sweetheart that the words were not original. If his sweetheart had her own valentine writer, she could search through it for the perfect answer to send back to her suitor. Do you think she would have told him where she had found her verse?

Heartless valentines

Before long, cards were printed especially for this day. The desperate boyfriend could now buy a beautiful valentine for his sweetheart. Not all the printed valentines contained sentimental verses. Some were funny. People sent these to their friends or family. Others were printed with cruel remarks on them. People sent them to acquaintances they disliked. Heartless valentines were often sent with no signature. People who are cruel are often too cowardly to face up to the consequences of their cruelty!

Commercial cards

Valentines came in all shapes and sizes. Sweethearts received imitation dollar bills with "I love you **this** much!" printed on them. Imitation telegrams were printed on pink paper and sent from addresses such as "Throbbing Heart Land." The dollar bill and the telegram valentines were soon banned because these imitations looked too close to the real things.

Some valentine cards were loaded with decorations. They had beads, seashells, fir cones, dried berries, and even artificial flowers attached to them. Perhaps you might make a three-D card for someone special next Valentine's Day!

Famous romances

"Famous Romances" is a Valentine's Day game. Each boy and girl is given a heart with the name of a famous man or woman. Players must find their mates. Examples of well-known couples might be Romeo and Juliet or Adam and Eve. "Romeo" must then search until he has found his "Juliet."

In later days, valentine cards, such as the one above, were bought instead of made by hand.

Poor Hector Humphrey! He has worked hard on his homestead, but has no one with whom to share his joys and sorrows. Hector is looking for a wife.

Tying the knot

A wedding was one of the most important social events for the early settlers. It took place in the afternoon. However, the wedding celebrations usually lasted up to a week.

Often the church was a long drive from the homes of the bride and groom. Sometimes this worked to the advantage of the bride! Read this story and see how one bride benefited by living a fair distance away from the village church.

The runaway bride

A young girl's father was anxious that his daughter marry a friend of his. Unfortunately for the young girl, the friend was an old widower. The young girl refused again and again to marry the old man. However, her father kept insisting. Eventually, the young girl agreed.

On the day of the wedding, the bride seemed surprisingly cheerful. Everyone assumed that she must have grown to accept the fact that she would marry the old widower.

The journey to the church began. The bride and her bridesmaids rode their horses ahead of the wagon which was carrying the old widower and the girl's father. The church was more than an hour's drive away.

After a short distance, the bride and her bridesmaids began to pull farther and farther ahead of the wagon. The groom did not worry because he knew that a horse being ridden always went faster than a horse pulling a wagon.

Foiled!

He should have worried! The bride had arranged to meet an old boyfriend on the way to the church. Her father and the unsuspecting groom drove patiently to the church. The bride and her boyfriend raced to the church and reached it half-an-hour before the others.

When the groom finally arrived at the church, he was astonished to see the bride and her new husband coming out of the church door!

Words about weddings

Some early settlements did not have wedding rings for sale in the stores, so the bridal couple had to borrow one for the occasion. They bought one of their own later.

Christmas was a popular time for weddings because the couple could be sure that all their friends were free to attend the important ceremony. During harvest, neighbors were simply too busy.

After a wedding, the bridal couple went for an afternoon drive around the country. They were trailed by a long line of buggies full of wedding guests.

One custom was to give a prize to the first person back home from the wedding. The groom tried to have the fastest horse so that he would win the prize!

The wedding cake was baked with a piece of nutmeg hidden inside it. The person who received the piece of cake with the nutmeg inside would be the next one to be married!

The young ladies took home a piece of the wedding cake and slept with it under their pillow. They believed they would dream of their future husband that night!

Sometimes mischievous boys stretched a rope across the road. When the wedding party arrived at the spot, they were unable to pass until they had given the boys a small "donation"!

A wedding dinner and dance was held in the evening. Sometimes the party lasted until daylight the next morning or even continued into the next night.

Charivari shenanigans

A **charivari** was an unwelcome addition to a wedding night. Neighborhood boys serenaded a newlywed couple with tin horns, horse or cow bells, fiddles, tin pans, copper kettles, or any other noisemakers they could find. The banging, clattering, ringing, and screeching usually took place late at night. It was impossible for the bridal couple to sleep.

The "musicians" sometimes blackened their faces and put their clothes on backwards. They wore horrible masks and strange feathered caps.

Paying for peace

What was the purpose of all this foolishness? Most of the time a charivari was a good joke on the couple and a good excuse for the guests to keep celebrating. The noise-makers demanded money or refreshments before they would stop their racket. When the couple did not give in to their demands, the noisemakers did not give up. The chari-vari was continued for several nights in a row.

Sometimes, however, a charivari was held by a community to show disapproval of a marriage. When a very old man married a very young girl or a recently widowed person married quickly after the spouse's death, the charivari was unfriendly rather than fun. Sometimes neighbors who were angry because they had not been invited to the wedding organized a charivari to take revenge.

Charivaris could be nasty. One group of troublemakers placed a board over the chimney and smoked the wedding couple out. In another community, neighbors broke into the house, seized the groom, and tarred and feathered him!

The church was filled with flowers on Easter. Beautiful voices filled the sweet air with harmony.

Easter festivities

Few of the settlers celebrated Easter as a holiday. They attended church, finished their daily chores, and then perhaps enjoyed a special meal in the evening.

The Dutch settlers first introduced Easter festivities to North America. They dyed eggs and scratched designs on the surfaces with sharp knives. Typical designs were tulips, hearts, butterflies, and, just for fun, elephants!

Busy bunnies

Easter customs began to spread across the country. Soon all the children knew that the Easter rabbit brought them eggs on Easter morning. The idea of an Easter rabbit came from the ages when the sun and the moon were thought to be gods. The rabbit played in the light of the white Easter moon and then brought colorful eggs, as bright as the sun, to good children. Children hunted for hidden eggs in their houses and gardens. It was a difficult task when the foxy rabbit hid the eggs in the hen house!

Decorating with eggs

When children discovered the eggs, they used them to decorate small evergreens or leafless trees. Children also tried to make Easter-egg birds. Very carefully, they made four holes in an egg shell. They made one for the head, two for the wings, and one for the bird's tail. The children put in an extra opening so that they could attach the bird to a thread and hang it up as a decoration. If children took care of their birds, they would last for years. Do you have the light touch needed to make an Easter-egg tree or bird? How long do you think your Easter-egg bird would last? Perhaps you could use it as a Christmas tree decoration the following December!

Is this the Easter bunny? The settler children kept rabbits as pets and were sometimes afraid that they might have penned up the one that brought them their decorated eggs!

The settlers met for an Easter picni[   ] *school yard. Notice the fancy Easter bonn*[   ] *ooks as though Jim might want to try o*[   ]

41

In later days, Easter became a more important holiday. The children in the picture, above, have just finished an Easter play.

Nothing is more fun than an Easter parade! I wonder why these girls don't think so?

Egging each other on

Easter became a day for Sunday school picnics and Easter parades. It also became a day for playing special Easter sports. Men and children challenged each other to see who could eat the most eggs. Would you like to compete in this kind of contest? Hard-boiled eggs were also rolled down a hill. The owner of the last uncracked egg was the grand winner of the competition.

A gooey game!

Another game that was fun but also very messy was throwing colored eggs into the air. Players tried to catch them before they hit the ground. If the egg broke in your hand it could be a little gooey! Nobody was afraid to risk getting splattered, however, because it was so much fun!

Cracking up

Children also armed themselves with as many hard-boiled eggs as they could. They tried to take only the eggs with the hardest shells. To test an egg for competition caliber, a child tapped both ends of the egg against his front teeth. When the competition began, one challenger held his egg in his open fist with his fingers around it like an eggcup. He supported his hand and the bottom of the egg with the palm of his other hand. The top of the egg was exposed to the enemy. The enemy's aim was to hit the top of the other player's egg with a strong egg of his own. The player whose egg cracked first had to give his egg to the winner of the egg fight. Each time a player won, he received another egg. What did he do with his winnings? He took them home to his family for breakfast the next morning!

Not all children played these egg games fairly. Some children made artificial eggs out of wood or marble. At first their competitors might be fooled. When the cheaters were discovered, however, it is easy to imagine what happened. Who would want to make a bunch of children angry when they were armed with eggs?

Whose egg is the hardest? Ready ... CRACK!

Hard-boiled beliefs

Settlers held a few curious beliefs about Easter. They thought that if eggs were laid on Good Friday and eaten on that same day or on Easter Sunday, the person who ate the eggs would have good luck for the rest of the year. They also believed that these eggs could be saved and used to cure many ailments. Look out if it rains on Easter Sunday! That meant that it would rain for the next seven Sundays in a row.

If there had been snow at Christmas, the settlers believed the snow would be gone by Easter. But the settlers believed that if there was no snow at Christmas, the children would have a hard time finding the Easter eggs hidden outside, especially if the eggs were not brightly decorated! Can you guess why?

43

The circus has come to town. Jill's father lifts her up so that Jill can see the strange sights. The townspeople will not get much work done while the circus is here. There are too many interesting attractions not to miss!

The circus comes to town

A traveling circus or **menagerie** brought great excitement to any town. A menagerie is a collection of wild animals on display. Traveling shows moved across the country, staying for a few days in each town. Settlers could not resist leaving their work. The attractions were like a magnet! The audience gazed open-mouthed at the weird costumes of the performers and caught glimpses of wild animals lurking in cages as the circus paraded into town. Settlers were eager to spend their hard-earned money in return for admission and a better look.

The circus was a riot of color and noise. The circus crier shouted encouragements, such as the following, at the crowd:

"Come and see the King of the lions from darkest Africa and a hyena all the way from Ethiopia! We have with us the ferocious panther or cougar of North America and even a pair of guinea pigs from the woods of Brazil and Patagonia. Have you ever laid eyes on the ribbon-nose baboon? Now may be your only chance! We even have Dandy-Jack the Semi-Equestrian riding in our show. Be sure not to miss it!"

Who was Dandy-Jack? Why, a monkey riding a pony, of course!

"What are you laughing at, boys?" asks the puzzled clown. "Don't you steer your donkey by his tail?"

45

Sally doesn't want to watch. Her pet turkey, Gobble, is going to be eaten for Thanksgiving dinner. Do you think Sally will be able to enjoy her meal?

*Don't look at me, turkey! It wasn't **my** idea to have you for Thanksgiving dinner!*

Thanksgiving

Thanksgiving celebrations were held to give thanks for the year's harvest. The harvest festival is one of the oldest celebrations in the world because all life depends on food and the harvest.

Many settler families were not able to have lavish celebrations but all made an effort to have a special dinner on Thanksgiving Day. Turkey, fresh vegetables, and fresh fruit were usually seen on the table. Families gathered together for this feast to give thanks for the blessings they had received.

46

These boys are getting a head start on the husking bee tomorrow. They will make corncob dolls with their sisters tonight.

Edible puppets

After Thanksgiving dinner, the settler children often played games or sports outside. They sometimes celebrated Thanksgiving by making puppets out of the gifts of the harvest. The children made a hole in a vegetable or a fruit. The hole was big enough to fit an index finger. The fruit or the vegetable was the puppet's head. The puppet's eyes, ears, nose, and mouth were made with a dull knife or a nail. The roots and greens of the vegetable or the leaves of the fruit decorated the puppet's head. A carrot top made a funny wig!

The children cut holes for three fingers in a piece of square cloth. They put the cloth around one hand, letting the index finger poke through one of the holes. The puppet head was placed on top of this finger and the bare finger that showed was the puppet's neck. The cloth wrapped around the hand was the puppet's clothing. Two fingers poked through the remaining two holes and waved around as arms!

Corncob dolls

Another common activity on Thanksgiving Day was to make corncob dolls. It was fun to paint a face on one end of the cob and then add some corn silk for hair. The rest of the cob was covered with the cloth. Children held the cobs underneath the cloth and poked two fingers through for arms. Would you rather make puppets out of vegetables and fruit, or dolls from corncobs?

47

Halloween high jinks

Halloween was not always as popular as it is today. In the early days only some English families celebrated Halloween. They had corn-popping parties, taffy pulls, and hayrides on Halloween. They spent an evening playing games such as **Apple Ducking.** Apples were placed in a large tub full of water and the competitor had to try to bite a chunk out of one of them. Often the only result was a soaking wet head!

Grandfather doesn't find apple-bobbing quite as funny as his grandchildren do!

Even a broom can be scary on Halloween!

Snap apple

Snap Apple was played by suspending an apple from a string and trying to bite it as it swung. Snap Apple was also played by attaching an apple to one end of a stick and a lighted candle to the other end. The stick was hung from the ceiling by a string tied to its middle and twirled. The object of the game was to bite the apple without being burned by the candle. Would you risk playing this game?

Fortune-telling seeds

When the apples used in the games had been eaten, their seeds were saved. When two boys were both fond of the same girl, they asked her to stick an apple seed on each of her cheeks. John chose the seed on the right cheek. Bill hoped for the seed on the girl's left cheek. If John's seed fell off first, he was miserable. He had lost his girl to Bill!

Children also played a second game with seeds. The seeds were labeled "home" and "travel." If the "home" seed was the first to fall from a person's cheek, the lucky child was assured a trip in the near future. If the "travel" seed fell first, the child had to be contented with the pleasures of home life.

Eerie faces

Children loved to carve frightening faces in pumpkins and then light them by placing candles inside the hollowed-out "head." The faces, which the early settlers children cut into their pumpkins, were not very different from the ones that children today carve into their jack-o'-lanterns.

Treats or tricks?

When the Irish settlers came to the New World, they brought with them the spirit and superstitions of Halloween that we still enjoy today. People believed that the spirits of the dead walked on Allhallows Eve. The custom of dressing in weird masks and costumes to go trick-or-treating came from these beliefs. What kinds of costumes do you think the settler children made? They did not have the materials with which to make fancy disguises. Which is the best Halloween costume that you have ever made?

Practical jokes went hand in hand with Halloween. Can you imagine building a fence across a road as a Halloween prank? Settler children hid their neighbors' animals, soaped the windows of houses and stores, and made scary noises in the dark. The people who were hurt by these "pranks" did not find them very funny!

Pussy-footing

What animal do you think of when you think of Halloween? A cat, of course! Here are some early superstitions about cats.

If a cat sits quietly beside you, it means that you will have peace and prosperity.
If a cat rubs itself against you, it means that you will have good luck.
If a cat jumps into your lap, it means you will have even greater good luck!
If a cat yawns, it means that you have neglected an opportunity.
If a cat runs away from you, it means that you have a secret which will be revealed within the week.

Scamp barks when he sees the ugly pumpkin face. He thinks the "monster" might harm his friends.

A lumpy pillow

In some parts of the country, settlers believed that on Halloween day you should walk out the door backwards and pick up some dust or grass. You should wrap it up in paper and put it under your pillow that night. You will dream of what the future holds for you.

Bread before bed

Some settlers also believed that if you ate a crust of dry bread before going to bed on Halloween, any wish that you made would be granted. How awful if you forgot to eat your bread crust! You would have to wait a whole year until you had another chance to make your wish come true.

Wonderful winter!

Winter was the season for pleasure. Although the settlers always had work to do, the hard labor of the harvest season was finished. There was more free time for recreation.

As soon as the weather got cold enough it was time for ice sports. When the ponds and lakes froze, both children and adults pulled out their skates. Skates made from wood and iron blades were strapped to boots. Some skate blades were made from beef bones!

Being a graceful skater was as important to the settlers as being a graceful dancer. The following was one settler's advice on the art of skating well.

Eleanor is not fond of the cold weather. In order to keep her warm, her friends have bundled Eleanor in blankets and brought hot tea along to make sure she stays that way.

Advice to skaters

"A good rider becomes part of his horse. His body follows the action of the animal. It is the same way with skating. Try to become part of your skates. Do not force your body to act against the skates."

Skaters were frequently warned about thin ice. Then, as now, many accidents occurred when careless skaters broke through the ice and fell into freezing water. Have you ever skated on a lake and seen a crack in the ice? What thoughts flashed across your mind?

The frozen pond became a place to meet during the winter. People held skating parties and found many ways to entertain themselves on skates. Adults pulled their friends across the ice on toboggans or sleighs. Boys made hockey sticks out of knobby, strong tree branches. They formed teams and tried to bat a ball around the ice.

Isabel and Amy wonder whether the pond is frozen. The weather has been mild lately. Amy tests the ice. Crack! How about snowshoeing instead?

51

Have you ever seen tobogganing chutes like these? These huge chutes of ice were built at winter carnivals. Different tobogganing teams raced each other. Oops! Something has gone wrong with the steering! Do you think the team still has a chance to win?

Have you ever seen such a long toboggan before? Do you suppose all these people will make it to the bottom of the hill together?

Sliding games

Sliding on ice was a simple pastime, but settler children made it into a real sport. Several sliding games were enjoyed by these rosy-cheeked youngsters. One was played on two parallel strips of ice. The sliders form a line. The best slider takes a run and slides down the strip. The other sliders follow in the same path. Each slider tries to touch the heels of the slider in front. If a slider does so, he or she is allowed to "go one up," which means taking the place of the slider in front. When the players reach the end of one line, the first slider leads the way back down the other line. Good sliders can work their way up the line to become leaders.

Knocking at the Cobbler's Door is a game played by sliding steadily along the ice on one foot while stamping on the ice again and again with the other foot.

Another trick is sliding backwards. If not done properly, this little trick can turn into quite a painful trip! Try sliding sitting down.

In the **Wounded Soldier,** the slider kneels on one knee while the leg is bent but with the foot on the ice. The slider tries to travel as far as possible in this position.

Snow play

No child can resist the lure of the snow when it is perfect for making snowballs and snowmen. Snowballs and snowmen were as common in the days of the early settlers as they are today. It was fun to see who could make the largest snowball. What hard work it was to push the monster around and around as it grew larger and larger!

Snow fights were also a great source of fun for the early settler children. They built forts of snow and had good-humored battles. When the game became too serious, it often ended by someone getting hurt. Playing in the snow is enjoyable when you do not have to worry about getting a snowball thrown at your head!

Struggle up ... Fly down!

Tobogganing and sledding have long been popular sports among children. Settler children spent many winter afternoons careening down the snowy hills. Tobogganing became so popular that people made artificial runs on the hills near some of the cities. Walkways were built beside the runs so the tobogganists and sledders could climb to the top to begin their runs. The courses were lit at night with torches and large lamps. Now that's life in the fast lanes!

Snowshoeing

Snowshoeing was an enjoyable sport as well as a useful way to travel across deep snow. Without snowshoes, walking across the country in the winter was often impossible. People formed snowshoeing clubs so they could enjoy hiking together.

Sleighs were not just for travel purposes. Some settlers liked to organize races across the fields or a snow-covered frozen pond. Notice how they bundle up to keep warm.

Dashing through the snow

The early settlers looked forward to winter because they could get out their sleighs. Travel was comfortable then because sleighs skimmed over the snow which covered the bumpy roads. Settlers visited people near and far, covering great distances with ease. The travelers bundled up in bear or buffalo rugs and set out, eager to see their friends and relatives. They were always sure of a warm welcome.

Many sleighs overturned on the snow-covered trails but there was little danger of anyone being seriously hurt. In the middle of the 1800s, one settler wrote in her diary:

"I have heard that it is a positive pleasure to be thrown into the deep snow, and John gave me the opportunity with an upset of the sleigh. I must say that the fall was soft and easy, but I was so enveloped in my long fur cloak that I scarcely knew how to get up again."

Iceboats also raced across the lake at great speeds, astounding the onlookers! Does this boat look like it is going quickly?

The Scottish settlers brought the sport of **curling** to this country. They made their curling "rocks" from wooden blocks. Curling rocks were later shaped out of actual stones. The curlers slid the rock across the ice toward a bull's-eye target painted on the ice. The aim was to slide the rock fast enough that it traveled across the ice but slow enough that it stopped in the smallest circle, the bull's-eye. The sweepers, who held brooms, swept furiously in front of the stone, smoothing the ice so the stone would reach the target.

Ice hockey was a very popular sport among young settler men. These hockey players do not have protective pads on. One slip on the ice, and ...

Hunting

Hunting for meat was an important part of the early settlers' struggle for survival. Boys were encouraged to practice shooting at targets. They learned to handle guns safely and to shoot accurately. Settler boys hunted for turkeys, partridges, and quails in the woods as well as for larger animals such as deer or bear. The early settlers depended on these sources of food to help them survive the winter months. They began their hunting careers by trying to shoot squirrels. Hungry settlers thought squirrels were "capital eating!" Boys were proud when they were skillful enough to bring home big game.

In the harvest months, guns and dogs were used to protect the corn fields from raccoons. Boys patrolled the fields, on the lookout for the black masks of the thieves.

A fowl deed

Wild pigeons and wild geese also destroyed the crops. The settler boys were in charge of ridding the fields of these pests. In the early days there were so many passenger pigeons that the branches where they rested often broke under the weight of the crowded birds. When the pigeons took flight, their vast numbers completely darkened the sky! The air was so thick with pigeons that settlers killed them by knocking them down with sticks! To the settlers it must have seemed as if there was an endless supply of passenger pigeons. Today, however, these birds are extinct.

There were many more wild animals in the early days than there are today. Hunters could often shoot their dinners from their doorsteps. It is hard for us to imagine killing for our dinner.

Tom looks forward to going hunting when he is older. Meanwhile, he pretends his pups are trained foxhounds ready to charge!

Hunting was not always a chore. Some men and women took pleasure in going on shooting parties.

*Some fish stories are just too far-fetched to believe. Can you write a short story about fishing? Pretend you are the shocked rider in this photograph. How big was **your** fish that got away?*

Fishing

Fish was a major part of the settler diet. Fortunately, fishing was a favorite pastime. Sitting under a shady tree or on a river bank with a fishing pole was a great way to work! People floating along in small boats or canoes was a common sight. After a hard day of work, the settlers liked to relax in their boats with their fishing rods dangling over the sides. Everyone enjoyed this restful, quiet hour on the lake.

Something's fishy

Often, spears or nets were used instead of fishing poles. One early settler used a unique method to catch pike. He shot his gun across the water. The fish rose to the surface of the lake with their bellies up. They were stunned by the loud sound of the gunshot! The fish remained in this sleepy state for a short time. The fisherman reached into the water and picked up the fish with his hand. He scooped as many fish as he could

into his boat. Finally, the remaining fish lying on the surface of the lake regained their senses and quickly swam away. Do you believe this strange tale?

Fish stories

Fishing was usually not that easy! One settler told this story:

"It was not always plain sailing with us, for Henry was so fierce in his thrusts that one night, when trying to spear a bass from his boat, he lost his balance with a jerk, and went into the water along with the spear, head over heels!"

The early settlers told as many tall tales about fishing as fishing fans do today. In 1782 a settler swore before the court of law that he had seen a mermaid in one of the Great Lakes! Can you beat that story?

On a sunny day, the beach is always crowded. Look at the huge waves. These daring young people are jumping right in. The beach is not only for the adventurous, however. Doris prefers to lie fully dressed under her umbrella. Can you imagine going to the beach or swimming with so many clothes on?

Around the branch and back again! Don't let your tub fill up with water or you may have to bail out!

Splish-splash!

Children were constantly given advice about how to swim because of the dangers of deep water. As with so many other activities, most children had to learn by doing.

Here is an example of a set of instructions for beginning swimmers:
1. Choose a safe place where the water is still and becomes deep gradually.
2. Wade out into the water until it is up to your neck.
3. Turn your face towards shore.
4. Shut your eyes and mouth, hold your breath, and plunge forward towards the shore, letting your head sink under the water.
5. Swim slowly and with the same kind of motion made by frogs when they swim.
6. When you have learned to swim under water, then try to keep your head out of the water by throwing it back. Do not raise your shoulders. In a little while you will find yourself able to swim quite well.

These school children are going for a picnic across the lake. They look forward to the boat ride, but are happy they do not have to row today. They are all dressed in their Sunday best.

Boating

Settlers who lived by a river or lake often owned boats. A boat was an excellent way to travel. Fishing was also easier from a boat. The pleasures of boating were discovered early. In their free time, the settlers jumped into their boats and paddled, rowed, or sailed simply for an hour's amusement.

As more and more settlers came to this country, they enjoyed large summer gatherings. Several neighboring families organized **regattas.** They met at a central point on a nearby lake. The fun started early. There were canoe races, sailing races, and swimming competitions. Regattas remained popular throughout the years. Eventually they became public affairs. Dances completed the day's fun.

Sheila was delighted when Phillip invited her for a ride in his boat. However, now she is a bit worried because she does not know how to swim.

59

Horsing around

Children loved to ride. They did not care if they had to ride the heavy old horses that pulled farm equipment. They flung themselves on the great broad backs of these workhorses. The huge horses plodded around the field with the children perched on top, holding the manes tightly.

Sometimes a settler family could afford a lively horse to pull their wagon and sleigh. The children loved to ride this horse which had more energy and spirit than the plow horses!

Prosperous settlers owned horses which were just for riding. Young people gathered on their mounts at a friend's house and then went for a ride together. They packed a picnic to eat for lunch. These holidays were rare because there was usually work to be done. Because it was a break from chores, a picnic ride was all the more pleasurable!

Children usually learned to ride without lessons. They simply learned by doing! Beginners gained many bruises in funny places from their first few attempts at riding!

A safe ride

One book written in the 1800s advised learners to practice their riding skills by using a chair. They were told to fasten a set of reins to the top of the back of the chair. They were then instructed to pull the reins just hard enough to raise two of the chair legs off the ground.

The trick was to keep the chair balanced on the two legs that remained on the ground. The exercise was thought to teach the beginner the right way to hold and pull the reins. It would probably have been simpler to ride a real horse than to do this chair exercise. Try it!

Runaway horse! Simon is trying hard to stay on top of the situation, as well as the horse!

Wealthy settlers learned to ride at special riding schools, such as the one in the picture.

Many people owned velocipedes instead of horses. The first velocipedes were made of wood and had no pedals. They were called "fast walkers" and were used for coasting down hills. Later velocipedes had bigger wheels and were made from iron instead of wood.

Susan has mastered her new velocipede.

Can you guess what is happening in this picture? These men are trying to convince the teacher at this velocipede school that they are ready to receive their "badges." Without badges, they were not permitted to ride on the streets. An out-of-control velocipede was dangerous to pedestrians.

Mavis has a guilty look on her face. Did she trip Gary, or was she just happy to see him fall after the way he was showing off?

It hurts to fall on the hard surface of the roller rink. These four friends hold hands as they learn to skate. Just look at little Marjorie! She certainly has no problems! What is Willie up to in the background? Is he inventing a new dance?

Rolling and bowling

Bob is writing up the score. He did not realize that his fiancée, Miss Hamilton, was such a good bowler. She has just bowled a strike, knocking down all the pins. Bob is glad that his wife-to-be is such a skillful competitor. Now he wishes that she were on his team!

Fair-weather games

Croquet was a popular settler game. Little Iris waits impatiently as the ground is cleared. She loves to watch her mother and father play croquet. Her nurse holds her back so that she does not get in the way of the scythe. The game finally begins. Aunt Carole tries a tricky shot. The gentlemen watch closely.

The battledores were made of wood. The shuttlecock was made of cork and feathers. The game of battledore was similar to the game we call badminton today. The rackets, or battledores, were much smaller than our badminton rackets. It must have been difficult to hit that bird!

Lacrosse was invented by the Indians. They played it to cure the sick or prevent misfortune. The settlers played the game for fun.

Cricket came to this country from England. This game looks a little like baseball. However, the rules are much different. Find out how to play it.

More fresh-air fun!

These naughty boys grew restless on a hot summer afternoon.   They played nicky-nicky-nine-doors on their neighbor. Mr. Steerforth is angry at the false knock.   Mary, however, seems more curious than displeased.

Hoopla!

One toy that every settler child longed to own was a hoop. Children took the iron hoops from old barrels and had hours of fun with them. Sometimes their father made them a wooden hoop as a special gift. A wooden hoop was a little easier to use than an iron one. The children rolled the hoop along the ground. To keep the hoop in motion, they tapped it with a stout stick. Sometimes a crook was used. A crook was an iron stick with a hooked tip. The children raced down hills with their hoops. The trick was to keep up with the hoops as they rolled faster and faster. The hoops might bump and take a wrong direction or simply fall over.

Hoop races

Children had hoop races across flat ground. The racers required speed and skill to keep their hoops moving. Some races involved running a short course with several sharp turns. Sometimes the competitors had to turn their hoops within a small circle marked out for the game. These feats failed without an experienced hand!

Another trial of skill was to see how many hoops one competitor could keep going at the same time. Some children could keep two or three hoops rolling at once. A few children could even keep four or five hoops rolling simultaneously.

Playing with hoops is a forgotten pastime. Perhaps you might like to try it. Be the first in your neighborhood to keep five hoops rolling at one time.

Skipping rope

Whenever children found a stray piece of rope, they kept it to use in their games. When you look into a school yard today, you see girls skipping rope. If you could go back to the days of the early settlers, you might be surprised to see that there were very few girls skipping rope. Usually boys played this game. The boys were warned not to skip with their shoes off because they would wear out their stockings too quickly! Skipping rope did not become a favorite pastime for girls until the 1830s.

Hopscotch

Early settler children played the game of hopscotch almost exactly as it is played today. The hopscotch outline was usually drawn in squares or rectangles. Sometimes triangles or even circles were used. The player threw the stone or "pitcher" onto the first square in a line. She hopped over this first square to land in the second. She continued up the series of squares, turned around at the top or sixth square, and came back down. She had to remain on one foot at all times.

The difference between hopscotch played now and hopscotch played by the settler children is that settler children did not pick up their stone when returning. They kicked it back to the start.

Not only children played with hoops. Bill teaches Rover how to leap through the hoop. Rover seems a bit uncertain of his ability!

Who'll buy a honey pot?

Honey Pots could be played either indoors or outdoors. The "honey pot" was a girl or boy rolled up stiffly with hands locked together under the knees. Two other players lifted the "pot" up by its arms and carried it around between them in a circle. They called out, "Who'll buy a honey pot?"

Sometimes the person being carried loosened her hands and let her feet drop to the ground before being carried all the way around the circle. If this happened, the fallen pot was required to pay a penalty.

I spy!

Does **I Spy** remind you of a game played today? Players marked a home base and divided into two teams. One team remained at the home base, eyes closed. The other team hid. After a length of time agreed upon by the players, the team on base yelled "Coming! Coming! Coming!" They tried to find the members of the other team. When a seeker discovered a hider, she yelled "I spy Mary Jones! Home for Mary Jones!" The seeker tried to rush to home base before she was tagged by Mary. If she succeeded, she was safe. If the seeker was too slow, she was put out of the game.

In another version of I Spy, a hider who was spied had to rush out and catch any one of the seekers. He then had to ride to home base on the seeker's back. Can you see any problems with this version of the game? In both versions, the game ended when all the hiders and seekers were at home base.

Give it a spin

Tops were fun to play with. They could be whittled from wood by clever fingers. Tops were large on top and gradually narrowed to the point on which they spun. The spin was started by wrapping a rope or "whip" around the groove carved around the middle of the top. The top would spin neatly away. One could do many tricks with tops.

Conqueror was a game in which each player tried to knock the opponent's top. A player needed a sharp eye, steady hand, and plenty of practice. If the top did not spin strongly, it toppled!

Dale and Clara make their little sister a kite for her birthday. All the children hope it is a windy day!

We'll race to the pine tree and back. Ready boys? On your mark, get set, GO!

Paul is upset because he has lost every single one of his marbles. Rick won the game fair and square. However, he hates to break the heart of his little friend. Do you think he will share some of his winnings with Paul?

Don't lose your marbles

Who would think that little glass balls could provide hours of entertainment? There were many different games played with marbles. The most popular game required that two circles be drawn on the ground, a smaller one inside a larger. Each player put a marble in the little circle. A player tried to hit the marbles in the center with his shooting marbles. His first shot was from outside the large ring. After the first shot, he took aim from the place where his shooting marble stopped.

If the player knocked a marble out of the ring, he could keep it. This was a good way of building up a supply of marbles! Look out, though! If a player hit another player's shooting marble, she was out of the game. She had to hand over all the marbles she had won in the game. Easy come, easy go!

The player who won the most marbles won the game. Of course, those who failed to knock their own marble out of the little ring before the game was over had a severe penalty to pay. They had to return all the marbles they had won plus an extra one for playing so badly!

Follow on

An easier game was **Follow On.** One player shot a marble and the second player had to hit the first marble with one of her own. This game was played in a lane or on a country road. If the second player missed her shot, the first player remained in front and shot his marble farther down the lane. If the second player ever succeeded in hitting the other's marble, she gained the forward spot. This game could go on as long as there was road left to play on.

Single hole

Another game played with marbles was **Single Hole.** The players made a small hole close to an old wall. A line was scratched in the ground less than an arm's length from the hole. The players decided how far away from the target they would stand. Each player contributed one marble. The first player took all the marbles and tried to throw them into the hole. He could keep all of the marbles that went into the target. All that fell between him and the line in front of the hole were "dead."

The player could hit the marbles that had fallen between the hole and the line. He used a flat stone or a piece of slate. If he hit a marble and knocked it into the hole, the marble was his. The next player gathered those that remained and tried her hand at the toss. The game continued until all the marbles were won or lost. It was no fun to lose all your marbles!

Everyone concentrates on this game of marbles.

Floral pastimes

In the days of the early settlers, the woods and meadows were overflowing with wild flowers. The variety of colors and the fragrant smells of these flowers were delightful to the settlers. The children did more than stop and smell the flowers. They put their imaginations to work and developed some fun activities based on the gifts of the nature around them.

Do you like butter?

A buttercup or dandelion was held under the chin of a friend. If there was a yellow reflection, it meant that the friend loved butter. This may be a trick that you have tried.

Then, as now, young children spent many sunny afternoons tying dandelions into chains. They called these pretty yellow necklaces "dandelion beads."

Bob makes a daisy crown for his sister. Frank uses a buttercup to test Lisa's love of butter.

When the dandelion season ended, the yellow heads of the dandelions changed into heads of down. The children took big breaths and puffed the "parachutes" with their seeds across the fields. When all the seeds blew off the stem, children believed their mother wanted them to come home. They also believed that they could tell time by counting how many seeds of fluff remained on the dandelion head after one puff.

"She loves me..."

Daisies were a favorite flower. A boy pulled off one petal, and said "she loves me." He pulled off the next petal and said "she loves me not." Whatever phrase he said when he plucked the last petal would be the verdict. You have probably tried this test. Does it work?

When the children spotted jack-in-the-pulpit flowers, they pinched the base of the flower. This made the inner spadix wiggle. "Jack" was preaching!

Children plucked broad leaves of grass and held them between their thumbs. They blew on them to make loud whistling sounds. This is still an easy way to make music! Reeds which grew near water made good fifes when holes were cut in their thick, hollow stems.

72

"Ladybug, Ladybug..."

When children saw a ladybug while they were wandering among the flowers, they called to it:

"Ladybug, Ladybug, fly away home;
Your house is on fire; your children will burn."

Have you heard this rhyme before? Some children still repeat it today!

Pine twigs with long needles were called "ladies" by the children. They trimmed the needles evenly. These were the ladies' "petticoats." The lady was placed upright on a piece of paper. The children blew on the lady to make her dance.

When the milkweed pods grew ripe and split, the little children believed they were fairy cradles. They put the silk of the milkweed into the empty pods to make tiny pillows for the fairies.

Flower petals made soft little skirts and bonnets for stick dolls. Acorns became cups and saucers. Dolls' clothes sewn from scraps of cotton were dyed with the juices of bright berries.

The settler children gathered and hoarded the horse chestnuts which fell from the trees. They peeled away the thick, bumpy shells which split when the chestnuts were ripe. Children loved the feel of the smooth, deep-brown chestnuts. Many chestnuts were kept simply because of their beauty. Children decorated their bedroom windowsills with the nuts. Some children used chestnuts and sticks or wire to make toy people and animals.

Settler children played a game called **cob-nut.** They tied chestnuts to the ends of strings. Two competitors aimed and swung their chestnuts, banging them together. The winner had the chestnut with the strongest shell. The shell of the loser's chestnut broke. Every child could play cob-nut because chestnuts were abundant.

Jennifer's basket is full of flowers but she finds it hard to stop picking them. Don't pick that one!

Every autumn brings new playthings. It's fun to dance in dry leaves!

73

Clara is losing the game! She cannot help smiling as Peter pinches her! Eileen hopes she isn't next!

The settlers brought the game of Blindman's Buff from Europe. This German family played it often before they emigrated. It remained their favorite game in the New World.

Parlor games

The parlor was the room where people spent their time after the day's work was done. Families and friends gathered there to play games. These indoor activities became known as **parlor games**. Settlers loved to play guessing games which tested their knowledge, but they also loved plain old shenanigans.

Pinch, no smiling!

Try one of their favorites, **Pinch, no smiling!** Everyone sits in a circle and each player pinches the nose of his or her neighbor. The first one to smile or laugh pays a forfeit. A forfeit was a penalty paid by the loser of a game. Often a forfeit was just a marker or toy. Each player would put one in the middle of the players' circle when she lost her turn or failed in her task.

At the end of the game, all the losers had to pay for their forfeits. Settlers dreamed up many ways to pay for a forfeit, such as answering questions while being tapped under the chin, imitating animals named by the other players, or hopping on one foot around the room. A player bought back a forfeit with a five-minute silence (no laughing!), by reciting poetry, or by repeating tongue-twisters. Paying for forfeits was often as much fun as playing the game!

Blindfolded fun

Even the settlers thought of **Blindman's Buff** as an old-fashioned game, but it always created new fun. Several players scampered around the room trying to escape the player who was blindfolded. The blindfolded player tried to catch and identify one of the players. The blindfolded player did not have an easy task. Have you ever wondered how this game got its strange name? Do you know what the word "buff" means? Buff is a short form of the word "buffet," which means to strike or blow. The "blind" player was certainly buffeted! The other players teased him by bumping into him and slipping away before he could grab them.

Some adults warned that Blindman's Buff was dangerous not only to parlors, but to people. They preferred **Silent Man's Buff** because the players had to keep still and silent while the "blind" person stumbled around the room and finally into a player. It was hard not to giggle and give yourself away when the "blind" player groped at your face. Hopefully, she would not poke her finger in your eye!

Jinglers and Um

Another kind of Blindman's Buff was **Jinglers.** One player carried a bell. The rest were blindfolded and chased the sound of the bell.

Um is another game in which a player is blindfolded. The other players sit on chairs in a half-circle. The blindfolded player plunks down on someone's knee, saying "Um." The seated player answers "Um" in a disguised voice. The blindfolded player may not touch the players with his hands. He must guess on whose lap he is sitting by the sound of that person's voice.

If the blindfolded player does not guess correctly after the other player has said "Um" three times, he must find another knee. If he does guess correctly, the blindfold is passed on to another player. All the other players change chairs and the game begins again. How good are you at disguising your voice? Could you fool the blindfolded player?

Richard has lost the game. He must now pay a forfeit. He strains his neck and bends it, trying to bite one of the cherries. John comes to check on Richard's progress.

MUSIC PLAYS.

NO MUSIC.

Playing Going to Jerusalem is fun. Walk until the music stops, then sit. These children also loved the games of The Post and Magic Music.

Musical chairs

Settler children often played Musical Chairs. One version of this game was called **Going to Jerusalem.** Another similar game was called **The Post.** All of the players except the Postal Clerk sit in two rows, facing one another. Each player chooses the name of a village, town, or city. The Postal Clerk writes down the names. When the Postal Clerk calls out "The post is going between Toronto and Boston," or any other two cities, the players with those names must change seats. The Postal Clerk tries to take one of those seats before the other player can reach it. Often the competitors end up sitting on top of one another instead of on the chair! When the Postal Clerk shouts "The general post is going out," everyone must scramble for a new seat. This is certainly a strange way to deliver mail!

Magic music

The settlers developed many talents that they could enjoy at home. **Magic Music** combined play and piano practice. One player leaves the room. The other players decide on a simple task that they want her to perform. They may want her to open a certain book. Magic Music is a game of trial and error. When the player returns, the piano is played so that the music tells the player what she is supposed to do. The music is played slowly and quietly to hint that the player is "cold," or not close to performing the correct task. When she begins to act correctly, she is "hot." The music is then played quickly and loudly. Can you play the piano? If not, there is another version of this game which you can play. Simply shout out "hot" or "cold" at the right time.

Settler children had many outlets for their creative minds. They loved to dress up in costumes and perform for their friends. Can you guess what story these children are acting out? Look carefully at their outfits.

The settlers loved the strange and unusual. A favorite pastime was watching a magic show. The quick hands of the magician amaze the audience. Even his two helpers do not know the secrets of the great Gonzo!

The noisy barnyard

The farmer in **The Barnyard** must be a good storyteller. The other players are assigned the names of animals in the barnyard. The storyteller begins her tale. During the story she will mention the names of as many animals as she can. When a player's chosen animal is mentioned, he must make the sound of that animal. A fast-talking farmer can cause the players to make quite a racket. Her story should include as many exciting and funny events as can be imagined. When the word "barnyard" is mentioned, the players must crow, moo, whinny, cluck, snort, and bay in chorus. Any player missing a cue pays a forfeit.

Earth, air, fire, and water

Even a handkerchief could become the focus of a game, as in **Earth, Air, Fire, and Water.** Everyone sits in a circle around one player, who throws a rolled handkerchief into the air, calling out the name of one of the four elements: earth, air, fire, or water. Earth is matched with "mammal," air is matched with "bird," and water is matched with "fish." The person who catches the handkerchief must at the same time shout out the name of a fish, mammal, or bird, depending on the element already named. When "fire" is called, the player who catches the handkerchief cannot say a word before she rolls and throws the handkerchief again. If someone yells "earth" and the catcher answers "eagle," he or she must pay a forfeit.

Puss in the corner

This game is played with as many players as there are corners in a room, plus one extra player who is the Puss. The other players are, naturally, the mice. The mice must switch corners swiftly enough that the Puss does not take one of their corners. Shy mice ruin the game. This is probably the only time your parents would ever want mice around the house!

Ten fine birds

How good is your memory? Anyone with a poor memory is sure to lose the game of **The Ten Fine Birds.** Again the players sit in a circle. One player starts by saying "A good fat hen." The phrase is repeated by everyone in the circle. Then the leader says "Two ducks and a good fat hen" and all the players follow suit. The game continues through the numbers until everyone must repeat this long list: "Ten bald eagles, nine ugly turkey-buzzards, eight screeching owls, seven green parrots, six long-legged cranes, five pouting pigeons, four plump partridges, three squawking wild geese, two ducks, and a good fat hen." Any player who forgets the list or makes a mistake must pay a forfeit. Try this game with the above list. Then try making up your own list. Be the leader in the circle. But remember, the leader must remember all the phrases so that the game will keep going!

Fly away, pigeon

Many games played by the settlers reflected their environment. Every day they saw dozens of different kinds of birds. In **Fly Away, Pigeon,** settler children and adults tested their bird-watching skills. The players sit in a tight circle around one player. The center player puts the forefinger of her right hand on her knee. The other players place their forefingers around hers. The center player calls "Fly away, pigeon," or "Fly away, sparrow," or substitutes the name of any other flying object. All fingers must be raised. When the center player names something that cannot fly, anyone who moves a finger must pay a forfeit. The game moves so fast that the players must be able to coordinate ears, thoughts, and fingers. In this game there is room for debate. Does a leaf fly? The person in the center must decide. We now have some flying objects that the settlers would not have known about. What might these be? Perhaps you can use them when you play Fly Away, Pigeon.

Buzz

Buzz is a counting game. The players sit in a circle. One player begins the game by saying "one." The next player says "two," and the counting continues around the circle until the number seven is reached. The word "buzz" is substituted for number seven and every other number with the digit seven in it. Any multiple of seven is also called "buzz." 70 is "buzz" because it is a multiple of seven. The player must say "buzz-one" for 71, and so on. A player who makes a mistake, either by saying the wrong number or forgetting to say "buzz," must drop out of the game. The last player left is the winner. You might like to play this game in math class.

Look at these crazy cats! They are the products of a settler child's imagination. The child is the storyteller in the game of The Old Family Coach. Her story began like this. "It was a cold snowy day when the wheels of the coach began turning. The doors began creaking, the harness began squeaking. The Pussycat Express was leaving town. Sitting on the crowded seats were a typical group of travelers, Kitty Kat, Tom Tabby, Big Al Lee, and little Baby Purr. The trip started out normally but ..." Take over from the storyteller and finish the game with your friends. Keep the other players jumping!

The old family coach

Enthusiasm and imagination were the key ingredients of the traditional settler games. The art of storytelling was learned during long winter evenings at the fireside. A good storyteller was needed for the game called **The Old Family Coach,** a game similar to **The Barnyard.** Each player takes the name of a part of the coach, whether a door, step, seat, window, coachman, horse or harness. The storyteller begins a wild story about the adventures of the coach, using the names of its parts as often as he can squeeze them in. Every time a

player's chosen part is mentioned, the player must stand, turn around, and sit down again. When the word "coach" is used, everyone must stand, turn and sit.

The game gets more exciting as the coach meets with disasters and survives narrow escapes. Any player who misses a cue pays a forfeit.

A similar game can be played by telling the story of a picnic. Imagine what could happen on a picnic with wasps, cows, ants, mustard, cheese, salt, pepper, salad, knives, forks, spoons...

Hunt the slipper

The players sit in a ring around the player who is "it." The player in the center gives a slipper to one of the players in the ring and recites this rhyme:

"Cobbler, cobbler, mend my shoe,
Get it done by half-past two."

The player in the middle turns his back and the other players begin to pass the slipper around the circle.

After a chosen length of time, the center player must begin by pointing at the player who he thinks is holding the slipper. When the player points at you, you must raise your hands. If you are caught with the slipper, you must go into the middle. Crafty players look guilty when they are innocent and innocent when they are guilty.

The players may continue to pass the slipper while the center player is guessing. They must be very careful to pass it only when the center player's back is turned. Would you be daring enough to throw the slipper across the room while the center player was not looking?

Jack straws

Jack Straws was a game that any settler child could play. All that was needed for this game was a large number of straws or fine splinters of wood. The pieces all had to be of equal length. The straws or splinters were placed in a pile shaped like a haystack or a tent. They met at the top and spread out at the bottom. The object of Jack Straws was to remove a straw or splinter from the pile without disturbing the others. If a player succeeded in taking a straw or splinter without jiggling the others, she counted one point. The next player would then try. The game continued until the stack fell. Then the number of

straws won by each player was added up. The winner was the player with the highest number of points.

Sometimes players blackened the heads of three of the straws or splinters with a piece of charcoal. These were called the king, queen, and bishop. These blackened pieces were worth extra points. The king was worth four points, the queen three points, and the bishop two points. The plain straws or splinters counted as one point.

Everyone wanted to pull out the blackened straws. Often an eager player risked the game trying for the king. The whole stack of straws fell!

This game can be played today by children with careful hands and a lot of patience. Try it with dry spaghetti. Play on a rug to keep the spaghetti from scattering.

Materials for Jack Straws were close at hand in the barn!

Me and my shadow

A piece of paper, a candle, and voilà, a shadow game! The settlers created interesting pastimes with next to nothing. A person sat in front of a candle. A profile would appear on a piece of paper which was fixed to the wall. Another person traced the silhouette onto black construction paper. The silhouette was then mounted on a piece of white paper. There are examples of silhouettes on this page.

A penny for a profile

Photography was invented in the middle of the nineteenth century. Before then, if people wanted a picture of themselves, they had two choices. They could hire an artist, which was very expensive, or they could have a silhouette-maker cut a likeness. Silhouette-makers were so skillful that they did not even have to trace the profiles first. They could simply trace the sitter's profile with their eyes while their hands cut the silhouette out of black paper.

A cheap man's art

Where did the word silhouette come from? People did not consider silhouette-cutters to be true artists. They felt silhouettes were very cheap art. That is why they were named after Etienne de Silhouette. He was a Frenchman who controlled the French government treasury. He was so cheap with his money that it was only fitting to have something cheap named after him! What would you like to have named after you?

Settlers were fascinated by shadows. When returning home late at night after telling ghost stories at a neighbor's home, the settler children were often frightened by the shadows of trees creeping along the road. However, when they were safe inside their homes, the settlers loved to use shadows in games!

Shadow buff

When playing **Shadow Buff,** a white sheet or tablecloth is hung in the room. One player stands in front of the sheet. The other players parade on the other side, between the sheet and a candle. Their shadows are thrown onto the sheet. The person in front of the sheet tries to guess who is on the other side. The settlers thought of ways to disguise their shapes and sizes in order to fool the player who was trying to guess their identities.

When the game of Shadow Buff is finished, the candle can be used for another game. One player is blindfolded and the candle is placed somewhere in the room at head level. The object of the game is to blow out the candle. The blindfolded player has to find the candle by following the shouted directions of the other players, such as "two paces backwards."

Would you like to have everyone laughing at you while you are huffing and puffing in all the wrong places?

Every settler child knew how to make simple **Hand Shadows,** but it was hard to find enough fingers to form the difficult ones! Here is an example of how to make a hand shadow. Can you make this shape appear on your wall?

At night, all shadows are scary!

Timothy found it easy to draw Louise's profile with the help of a candle. Try it yourself! Use a flashlight instead, for safety's sake.

Indoor projects

John and Mary built this doll house for their younger sisters. They all enjoy playing in it. It even has a second story!

Store-bought toys were a luxury. Most settler children had only homemade toys, but they did not mind. They discovered that homemade toys were as much fun to make as to use. China dolls bought from city stores were cherished, but dolls made out of sewing scraps were just as special. Children were proud of their skills, not just of their possessions. They learned to be little carpenters, building and furnishing gorgeous doll houses. Every detail was carefully added, from fringes on curtains to flowered wallpaper.

Cat's cradle

Making the game of **Cat's Cradle** was as simple as tying the ends of a long piece of string. Two players looping this string around their fingers could turn the string into a cradle, a cross, a diamond, or a spider's web.

The thaumatrope

An interesting toy was a **thaumatrope**, a word which is made of two Greek words meaning "wonder" and "to turn."

To make a thaumatrope, take a piece of cardboard about twelve centimeters by eight centimeters. On one side paint a black horse running against a white background. On the other side, paint a person sitting upside-down and holding a long pole with a carrot at the front end.

Fasten two pieces of thread in the middle of each side of the card. When the threads are held between the thumb and forefinger of each hand and the card is twirled around, the person will seem to be riding a horse.

The settlers did not know about films. However, the thaumatrope showed them that moving pictures were a future possibility.

See what other moving pictures you can construct using this easy method!

Sundials

Making a sundial is an easy job and a useful activity. When you finish, you can tell time with your toy. Take a square piece of stiff cardboard. With a compass, draw as large a circle as will fit in the square. Draw another circle just inside the first circle. Draw a third circle as shown in the diagram. Divide the rings between the first and third circles into twelve equal parts, as in a clock. There are twelve parts in the "ring" formed by the two largest circles. Divide each of these parts into five little sections. Now you have the face of a sundial.

With a sharp knife and a ruler, cut a slit in the face of the dial from the center to the number twelve. Cut a triangle with a 45-degree angle from another piece of cardboard, leaving a flap, as shown below.

Insert the flap into the face of the sundial with the tall end at twelve. Bend the flap, and tape or glue it underneath the sundial.

Set your sundial outside so that at noon there is no shadow falling on the face of the dial. The number XII should be the farthest point away from the sun. If your sundial is positioned correctly, the shadow will fall clockwise around the dial as the sun moves. The shadow will indicate the correct hour.

If you ever find yourself on a desert island, you can make a sundial by drawing a circle in the sand and planting a stick in the center of it. Mind you, why would you need to tell time on a desert island?

Feather baskets

It was easy for settler children to collect enough feathers to make a basket. If they could not find enough feathers from the wild birds in the forest, they could simply pay a quick visit to the chicken coop!

To make a feather basket, cut a circle of cardboard and punch holes around the circumference. Cut off most of the quill ends of the feathers and stick the feathers through the holes. Twist a piece of wire into a circle a little larger than the cardboard base. Cover the wire with wool or some other material. Attach the wire to the inside of the feathers, near the tips. This will be the rim of the basket. A handle can also be made of covered wire.

Paper puzzles

The settlers could combine their imagination with almost any object and invent a game! Paper was cut to make puzzles. Here is an example of a paper puzzle.

Draw twelve holes onto a square piece of cardboard in the following pattern:

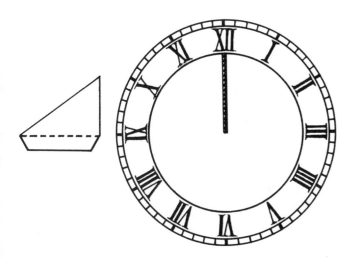

0	0	0
0	0	
0		0
0	0	
0	0	0

See if you can cut the paper into four pieces of the same shape. Each piece must have three holes in it. See page 94 for solution.

The magic lantern was a special toy. Children were allowed to stay up until dark in order to see a magic lantern show. The excitement kept their eyes wide open!

Magic lanterns

Magic lanterns were like slide projectors, but not nearly as complicated. The magic lantern was a box in which a candle was placed. The box had a chimney to let the smoke out and a tunnel on one end through which the candlelight shone. Children made their own slides. They painted brightly colored squares of glass. They also drew pictures on slides by holding the pieces of glass over a candle flame until the glass turned black. A sharp stick was used to scrape the picture into the black soot. It was easy to cut out silhouettes in black paper and paste them on the slides. Everyone's favorite slides were those that told a story about a family. The homemade slides were held in front of the magic lantern's small beam of light. The images on them were enlarged by the light and projected onto the wall.

Illuminating

Illuminating books was a creative pastime on rainy days and Sunday afternoons. Children carefully decorated, with silver or gold paint, the capital letters of the words starting the chapters or paragraphs in books. You may have noticed old books with scrollwork on and around the letters. These were done by professional illuminators.

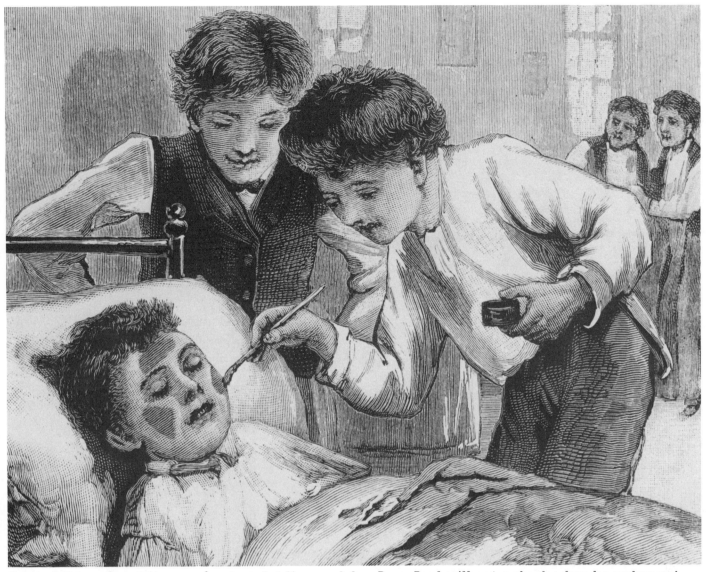

Some children found it more fun to paint live models. Poor Paul will get a shock when he wakes up!

Spatterwork and outlines

Spatterwork was a good way to fritter one's time away. You may have tried spatterwork yourself. Objects with pretty shapes, such as a fern picked in the forest, were pinned to a large sheet of paper. India ink or colored paint was sprayed on the paper with a toothbrush rubbed against a comb. When the fern was unpinned, its shape was left amid the spatters of ink or paint.

Outlines was a challenging drawing game. One person drew a simple line or shape. Another person had to draw a picture by adding onto the first line or shape. If the first line was straight, it was easy to make a picture from it. A figure eight was a little more challenging. The player drawing had to work quickly. The lines and pictures had to be varied. The worse the picture, the funnier the game!

More creative fun

Children also enjoyed copying drawings like the ones found in this book. They used a tiny quill pen and India ink. You could try this with a sharp pencil. Keep an eraser handy for correcting mistakes.

For a more "down to earth" activity, children dug up muddy clay from the garden and used it for sculpting all kinds of objects. They would leave the works of art to harden in the sun. Can you imagine the types of articles or toys they might have molded?

When illustrated newspapers became common, children snipped pictures and stories for scrapbooks. This is an activity that you might find both educational and interesting. Pick a theme and illustrate it with pictures and stories from newspapers or magazines.

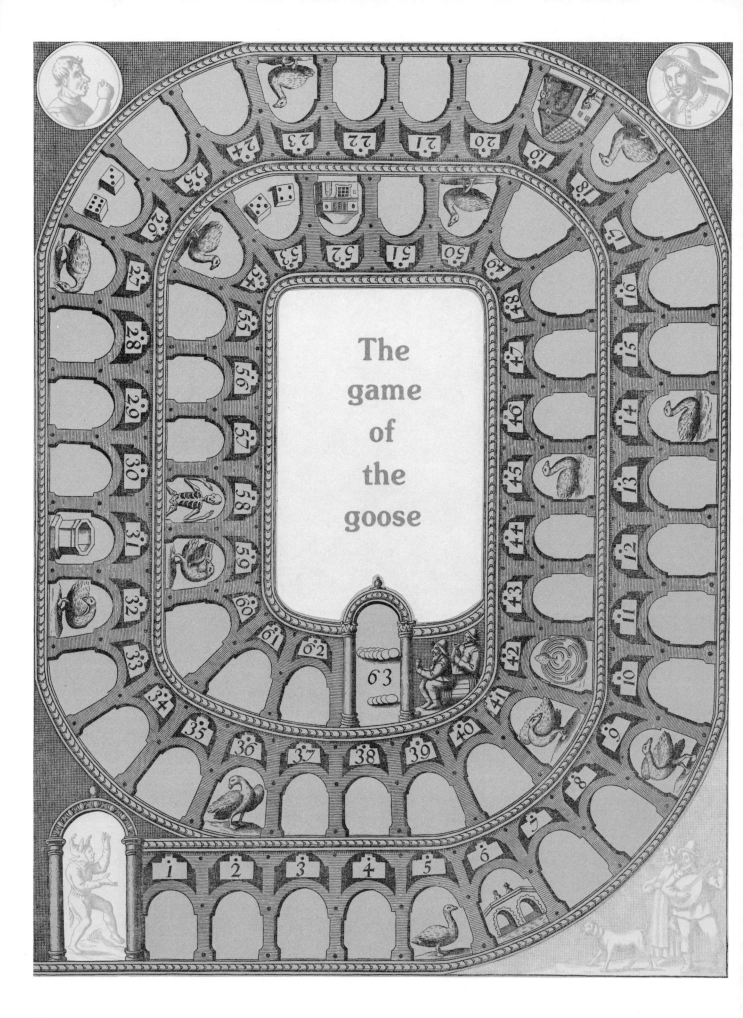

The game of the goose

In the early days, settler children took such good care of their board games that they could pass them on to their children. Board games often could not be replaced because not very many copies were printed.

The Game of the Goose was an old board game played in England and Europe before the settlers brought it to the New World. Both adults and children loved this game of chance. The goose has always been a popular animal in games, stories, poems, and sayings. Mother Goose is the queen of nursery rhymes.

The story of the goose that laid the golden egg was first told by a Greek man named Aesop. Aesop wrote his **fables** more than 2,000 years ago. Do you know this old story? The fable tells of a stranger who gave a married couple a goose that laid a golden egg each morning. The couple lived a good life. They had been very poor but soon became rich. Unfortunately they also became greedy. They decided to cut the goose open so they could get all the golden eggs at once. They chopped off its head and found it was a plain old goose. They soon became poor again because, in their greed, they had killed their source of golden eggs.

The object of the Game of the Goose is to be the first to reach the golden eggs in square 63. You need counters, five stakes, and a pair of dice. Settler children used fruit seeds as counters and pieces of straw for stakes. See what you can find. Two or more players may play this game. Each player donates one stake before the game begins. Counters are put on the joker, which precedes square number one. Each player rolls the dice. The player with the highest throw takes the first turn and the dice are passed to the left.

Here are the rules you must know before you start to roll:

1. If you land on a square already occupied by another counter, both players must pay a stake. Then the counters exchange places, even though the first counter got there first!

2. If you land on one of the 13 squares with a goose, you have a choice. You may take one stake from the pile and remain on that square, or pay one stake into the pile and move your counter twice as far as your roll. There is one exception to this rule. If you throw a nine and land on a goose, you may not double your throw. If you land on a goose and then throw a nine, you may not double your roll. If you examine the board, you can see that you would move by 9 x 2 or 18 and land on another goose. Again you would double your roll and land on yet another goose. This would continue until you landed on 63 and won the game. This would be a very short game and not much fun for the other players.

3. Any other squares with pictures are **hazards.** Here is an explanation of what happens when you land on the different hazards.
i   The Bridge. To cross the bridge, number 6, you must pay a toll of one stake and move to number 12.
ii   The Inn. When you arrive at the inn, number 19, you pay for a meal with one stake and lose one turn while you are eating it.
iii   The Dice. If you land on the pair of dice, number 26 and number 53, you must pay one stake and move back nine spaces. If this lands you on an occupied square, both players pay a stake. Do not exchange places.
iv   The Well. If you fall into the well, number 31, you must pay a stake. You lose two turns while you are climbing out. If another player happens to land on the same square, you are rescued and leave him behind to wait two turns.
v   The Maze. When you get lost in the maze, number 42, you must pay a stake and go back to number 29.
vi   The Prison. When you land in prison, number 52, you must pay a fine of one stake. You remain there until another player bails you out by landing on the same spot.
vii   Death. Pay a stake if you land on number 58. Your goose is cooked! But all is not lost. You can begin life again at square 1.

4. If you run out of stakes during the game, you are out. In order to win the game, a player must roll the exact number of squares needed to land on number 63. If you throw more than you need, you must move backward. The first player to land on square 63 is the winner.

These girls are counting-out. None of them wants to be "it"!

Word games*

Words, words, words! Settlers used them with skill and delight. Tongue-wagging was a wonderful pastime. Trying tongue-twisters tests talent:

"Theophilus Thistledown, the successful thistle sifter, in sifting a sieve full of un-sifted thistles, thrust 3,000 thistles through the thick of his thumb."
Say this five times as fast as you can!

Invite your friends over to try some of the settlers' favorite games. Try a rhyming invitation, such as the following one that a settler girl sent to her friends:

"Pack up your trunk, let's see your face,
You'll find a welcome at this place."

Counting-out rhymes

Rhymes were used to decide turns or who would be "it." Here are some samples of counting-out rhymes. They do not make much sense, and they are not supposed to!

One–ery, two–ery

One-ery, two-ery, ichery, Ann;
Hollow-bone, crackabone, ninnery, tan;
Spittery spot, it must be done,
Tweedledum, tweedledum, twenty-one.

Intry, mintry

Intry, mintry, cutry, corn,
Briar seeds and apple thorns,
Briars, wire, limber lock,
Five geese in a flock,
Sit and sing,
By the spring,
O-u-t and in again.

O–U–T and you are out!

He had money and I had none,
And that was the way the quarrel begun
As O-U-T, out!

What counting-out rhymes do you use?
Do they make any more sense than these?

Puzzling it out

The settlers enjoyed proverb puzzles. Prov-erbs are old sayings such as "Better late than never." The following letters must be rearranged to form a well-known proverb:

a b eee f k ll oooo p r u y

Here is one last puzzle. Can you figure out how to read it?

stand	take	to	taking
I	you	throw	my

Having trouble? Here is a hint. You must pay attention to where the words are located in relation to each other. The words are not beside each other. Where is the word "I" in relation to the word "stand"? Now try the puzzle again.

By me all the young are beguiled,
I puzzle man, woman, and child,
I make everyone try his brain,
But often the brains work in vain;
And yet I am plain there's no doubt,
And simple enough when found out!

The answer is, "A riddle." Settlers loved
them. Here are some others for you to
try.

More riddles

Two brothers we are,
Great burdens we bear,
By which we are bitterly pressed.
In truth we may say,
We are full all the day,
But empty when we go to rest.

My first carries my second,
My third carries them both,
And my whole is a useful accomplishment.

My first marks time,
My second spends it,
And my whole tells it.

My whole's a term the world directs,
The use of to the female sex;
Dismiss a letter and you'll find,
The first that lived of human kind;
Dismiss another and you'll discern,
What causes mill wheels to turn;
Again dismiss one, and you'll see,
The first tense of the verb "to be,"
And last of all you'll read my name,
Backward or forward still the same.

If you are having trouble, here is a hint.
The answer to the first clue is a five-letter
word. The answer to the next clue is four
letters. The answers keep getting smaller.
The answer to the last two lines is the same
as the answer to the first clue. If you cannot
get the clues in order, begin at any one
of them. Once you have one answer, the
rest will be easy to guess.

The following riddle hides a girl's name
somewhere in the sentence.
Did you ask him if he lent George his book?
Can you invent sentences in which the names
of your friends are hidden?

Hmm...that's a tricky riddle.

Settlers loved riddles so much that they
played a game making them up. One player
takes a piece of paper, writing down any-
thing that comes to mind. As an example,
let us say, "A riddle." The paper is folded
and passed on. Another player writes his
or her first thought. Suppose she writes
"A rock." The third player combines the
two words in a riddle, saying, "Why is a
riddle like a rock?" The players must come
up with a sensible answer. One answer could
be, "Because they are both hard."

Metagrams

This riddle using letters is called a **metagram.** "Meta" is a prefix taken from the
Greek language. It means "change." "Gram"
is also from a Greek word. It means "letter."
You will see why this riddle is called a metagram.

I am a writing utensil.
Change my head and I am a bird.
Again change it, and I am a boy's name.
Again, and I am an animal's home.
Again, and I am a number.

Are you having trouble? Here is a hint.
"Change my head" means change the first
letter of the word.

*See page 94 for answers.

Perhaps you will not laugh at the old jokes below, but this trio certainly found them amusing!

Funny bones

What is the difference between a man
in deep thought and King Henry VIII?
One is a fat king and the other is a thin-king.

How many sides has a plum pudding?
Two — inside and outside.

Why is a dog like a tree?
Because both lose their bark when dead.

What word is that of which, if you take
away the first letter, all will still remain?
Fall.

What should you keep after you have given
it to another?
Your word.

A little girl wanted to say that she had a
fan, but had forgotten what it was called;
so she described it as "a thing to brush the
warm all off of you with."

The gardener's motto: "Lettuce plant."

"Papa, are you growing taller all the time?"
"No, my child, why do you ask?"
"Because the top of your head is poking
up through your hair."

A lady was lately hugged to death. Another
illustration of the power of the press.

A writer on school discipline says, "Without
a liberal use of the rod it is impossible to
make a boy smart."

A romantic young man says that a woman's
heart is like the moon — it changes continu-
ally, but always has a man in it.

A veteran shoemaker says that although
his clerks are very talkative during the day,
they are always ready to shut up at night.

A hearty gentleman — Sir-loin
A positive gentleman — Cer-tain
A suspicious gentleman — Sur-mise
A cowardly gentleman —Sur-render

Little Bobby was pulling the dog's tail, when
his aunt said: "You musn't do that, Bobby.
He will bite you."
"Oh, no," said Bobby, "dogs don't bite at
this end."

Joy: Where were you born?
Joshua: In North America.
Joy: What part?
Joshua: All of me.

"What's the child's name?" asked the clergyman of the grandfather at the christening.
"I dunno," the grandfather replied. And
he turned to the father and whispered
hoarsely: "What's the name?"
"Hazel," replied the father.
"What?" asked the grandfather.
"Hazel," repeated the father.
The grandfather threw up his hands in disgust.
"What do you think of that?" he asked the
clergyman. "With all the girls' names there
are to choose from, and he had to name
her after a nut!"

*What this group needs is a good laugh! Do you
think the jokes on this page could coax a smile
or two?*

Smith and Jones were discussing the question
of who should be the head of the house, the
man or the woman.
"I am the head of my establishment," said
Jones. "I am the breadwinner. Why shouldn't
I be?"
"Well," replied Smith, "before my wife and
I were married, we made an agreement
that I should make the rulings in all major
things, my wife in all the minor."
"How has it worked?" queried Jones.
Smith smiled. "So far," he replied, "no major
matters have come up."

Madge: Why don't you think before you
speak, dear?
Paul: If I did that, I shouldn't have time to
say half of what I wanted to say.

Doris was radiant over a recent addition
to the family and rushed out of the house
to tell the news to a passing neighbor.
"Oh, you don't know what we've got upstairs!"
"What is it?"
"It's a new baby brother!" And she settled
back upon her heels and folded her hands
to watch the effect.
"You don't say so! Is he going to stay?"
"I expect so" — very thoughtfully — "he's got
his things off."

Frank: My teacher was angry at me today.
Father: Why was that?
Frank: I told her that I didn't know where
the Great Lakes were.
Father: Next time remember where you put
things.

Here is one puzzle we could not answer! What is happening in this picture? Why does the man have his wig off? What is he reading? Why is the old woman angry? Who is the younger woman? What is your solution to this puzzle?

Answers to puzzles

p. 85 **Paper puzzles** solution

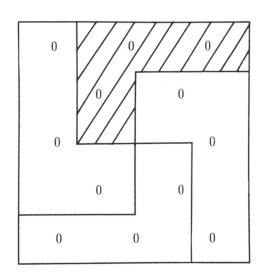

p. 90 **Puzzling it out** solutions

a b eee f k ll oooo p r u y
Answer: Look before you leap

p. 90

stand	take	to	taking
I	you	throw	my

Answer: I understand you undertake
to overthrow my undertaking

p. 91 **more riddles** solutions

Two brothers we are ...
Answer: shoes

My first carries my second ...
Answer: horsemanship

My first marks time ...
Answer: watchman

My whole's a term ...
Answer: madam

Did you ask him if she lent George
his book?
Answer: Helen [he len(t)]

p. 91 **Metagram** solution

I am a writing utensil ...
Answer: pen, hen, Ben, den, ten

94

Glossary

barter *to trade one thing for another without using money*

battledore *a paddle or racket used to hit a shuttlecock over a net*

beau *a sweetheart or boyfriend of a girl or woman*

bee *a gathering or meeting of people that combines work with pleasure*

blacksmith *a person who makes things out of iron*

chaperone *an older woman who acts as a companion for a young unmarried woman when she is with a young man*

charades *a game in which words or phrases are acted out silently*

charivaree (shiv-a-ree) *a noisy celebration held in honor of a newly married couple*

cob-nut *a large egg-shaped nut from a type of hazel tree; also, a game played with cob-nuts*

cricket *a game played between two teams using a ball, bat, and two wickets (sets of wooden stumps)*

croquet *a lawn game in which wooden balls are knocked through hoops with a large mallet (a long hammer with a wooden handle)*

crossroad *a place where two or more roads meet*

curling *a game played between two teams in which large stones are slid over ice at a target*

emigrate *to leave one's own country to settle elsewhere*

excursion *a short trip taken for pleasure*

fable *a made-up story, often including animals, that teaches a lesson. Aesop's Fables are famous example of fables.*

fife *a musical instrument similar to a flute but smaller*

foal *a young horse, donkey, zebra, or other member of the horse family*

forfeit *something given up or paid as a penalty*

gristmill *a mill that grinds grain into flour*

hazard *a risk; a chance of danger*

homestead *the house, land, and buildings where a family makes its home*

husking *removing the outside covering (the husk) from corn*

India ink *a thick black ink used in drawing or in printing signs*

inquisitor *a person who searches for information about someone by asking many questions*

jack-in-the-pulpit *a tall plant with tiny flowers found inside a leaf that is shaped like a hood*

journal *a book for keeping a daily record*

lacrosse *a field game in which two teams use sticks with nets to catch or throw a rubber ball*

lozenge *a small piece of candy or a tablet of medicine*

magic lantern *an early kind of projector for showing slides on a screen or wall*

menagerie *a collection of wild animals kept in cages for exhibition*

Methodist *a member of a church that began in England in the eighteenth century*

milkweed *a weed whose stem contains a white juice that looks like milk, and whose pods open to release seeds that look like tiny soft feathers*

mummer *a person who acts or plays in a mask or costume*

nineteenth century *the years 1801 to 1900*

nutmeg *a seed, used as a spice, that grows in the tropics and is about as big as a marble*

pantomime *a play without words, in which the players use body movements to act out the story*

Patagonia *a dry, grassy region in southern South America*

polluted *made dirty with harmful chemicals, gases, or other wastes*

potluck dinner *a party at which each guest brings a different dish of food*

prefix *one or more syllables placed at the beginning of a word to change its meaning. In "unhappy," "un" is a prefix that means "not."*

produce *fresh fruit and vegetables*

profile *a side view, usually of a human face*

reel *a lively folk dance performed by two or more couples*

regatta *a boat race or a series of boat races*

sampler *a piece of cloth embroidered with designs or words*

scrollwork *fancy, spiral-like writing*

sculpting *making figures or shapes (sculpture) from stone, metal, clay, or wood*

scythe *a tool with a long curved blade attached to a long bent handle. A scythe is used to cut down grass or grain.*

settlement *a small, fairly new community or village*

shenanigans *nonsense or mischief*

shuttlecock *a rounded piece of cork or other material with a crown of feathers*

smart *to feel or cause a sharp pain*

sophisticated soirée (swa-ray) *an elegant party given in the evening*

spadix (spay-diks) *the tiny flowers found inside the leaf of a jack-in-the-pulpit and other plants*

sparking *courtship; romance*

spooning *showing tenderness and love, sometimes in a silly way*

stake *something that is risked in a game*

stone-putting *throwing heavy stones or weights from the shoulder*

suitor *a man who seeks the love of a woman*

superstition *a belief that one action will cause a second action not related to it. Believing 13 to be an unlucky number is a common superstition.*

tar and feather *a cruel and painful punishment. Heated tar was poured on a victim who was then covered with feathers.*

treasury *the place where the money of a government, club, or company is kept and paid out*

threshing *separating the grain or seeds from wheat*

velocipede *an early form of bicycle or tricycle*

veteran *a person who has had much experience in a certain occupation or task*

zither *a musical instrument that is made of a shallow box with 30 to 45 strings stretched over it*

Index

Acknowledgements

Library of Congress, Dover Archives, Colonial Williamsburg, Century Village, Lang, Upper Canada Village, Black Creek Pioneer Village, Metropolitan Toronto Library, Colborne Lodge, Toronto Historical Board, Gibson House, City of Toronto Archives, Bibliotheque National du Quebec, Harper's Weekly, Canadian Illustrated News, Public Archives of Canada, Notman Photographic Archives, Little Wide Awake, Frank Leslie's Illustrated Magazine, the Osborne Collection of Early Children's Books, Toronto Public Library, the Buffalo and Erie County Public Library Rare Book Department, Jamestown, Chatterbox, McCord Museum, Harper's Round Table Magazine, John P. Robarts Library.
456789 BP Printed in Canada 098